WINNING WITH PURPOSE

Raising Our Game and Lifting Our
Teammates, On and Off the Court

Satch Sullinger
with John Dauphin

Foreword by Clark Kellogg
Afterword by Jared Sullinger
With a Special Message from Dick Vitale

"Winning with Purpose is a great read, especially in helping players and their parents understand what true team success really means. Coach Sullinger reminds us here that, while talent is important, it is nothing unless accompanied by quality character. This is a lesson for a lifetime!"

—Gary Williams, former head basketball coach,
University of Maryland

"Winning with Purpose illustrates in compelling fashion the important parts ... accountability, integrity, collaboration and commitment that play in our ability to succeed in the game of life. This book is a motivational gem!"

—Nneka Ogwumike, 2012 WNBA Rookie of the Year,
Los Angeles Sparks

"Coach Sullinger's message in *Winning with Purpose* about what it takes to support success by young people, in our community and across the country, should serve as an example to all of us who work to help kids achieve great futures."

—Rebecca Asmo, executive director,
Boys & Girls Clubs of Columbus

"Satch Sullinger is one of the greatest people I have been fortunate to work with in all my years around the game!"

—Bill Wall, former executive director, USA Basketball

WINNING WITH PURPOSE

Raising Our Game
and
Lifting Our Teammates,
On and Off the Court

by Satch Sullinger
with John Dauphin

Foreword by Clark Kellogg • Afterword by Jared Sullinger

Requests for permission should be addressed Ascend Books, LLC, Attn: Rights and
Permissions Department, 12710 Pflumm Rd., Suite 200, Olathe, KS 66062.
10 9 8 7 6 5 4 3 2 1

Printed in the United States of America
ISBN- 978-0-9889964-6-5
ISBN: e-book 978-0-9889964-7-2

Library of Congress Cataloging-in-Publications Data Available Upon Request.

Publisher: Bob Snodgrass
Publishing Coordinator: Beth Brown
Editor: Cindy Ratcliff
Dust Jacket and Book Design: Cheryl Johnson
Sales and Marketing: Lenny Cohen, Dylan Tucker

All photos courtesy of Satch Sullinger unless otherwise indicated.

Every reasonable attempt has been made to determine the ownership of copyright.
Please notify the publisher of any erroneous credits or omissions, and corrections will be
made to subsequent editions/future printings. The goal of the entire staff of Ascend
Books is to publish quality works. With that in mind, we are proud to offer this book to
our readers. Please note, however, that the story, the experiences and the words are those
of the author alone.

Printed in the United States of America

www.ascendbooks.com

To Barbara, who has always been there for me and is an incredible mom to our sons.

To J.J., Jules and Jared, who make me feel like the luckiest father in the world.

And to my Grandpa Jim and Coach Pat Penn, whom I wish were here to read these pages.

CONTENTS

FOREWORD

by Clark Kellogg

Through the game of basketball, God has granted me the privilege of meeting lots of special people over the last four decades—coaches, players, administrators, officials, parents and media. All have blessed me one way or another. Some have been pleasant acquaintances. Some have been mentors. Many have become friends. I consider Satch Sullinger a friend, kindred spirit and mentor. His example of caring and sharing is admirable and inspirational to me.

I don't recall specifically when Satch and I first met, but I know it was over twenty years ago, and centered on basketball. I do recall, however, that I liked Satch instantly and was drawn to his "presence." His size, demonstrative personality and constant, colorful chatter command attention. But that was only part of it.

Satch's passion, sincerity and respect for the game of basketball were striking to me, as was his love of people, particularly kids. We share much common ground there. His knowledge of the game and dynamic way of explaining and teaching its fundamentals is direct, effective and sprinkled with humor. It is those attributes that enable Satch to connect with players and parents alike, to teach valuable life lessons through the game of basketball to anyone he meets. As a former player, high school and college coach, and father of three sons who played college basketball, his perspective on how the game should be played and taught is powerful. With three children of my own who were college athletes, also, I believe in Satch's strategies for success on and off the court.

In *Winning with Purpose*, Satch pulls no punches where teamwork, discipline and doing things the right way are concerned. In candid and disarming fashion, he offers "real talk" for coaches, players and parents. Drawing from his own trials and triumphs, Satch lays out clearly the foundation for living a life *of* purpose, *on* purpose, no matter our circumstances.

Satch speaks here to the positive impact others have made in his life through playing with purpose and embraces the opportunity and obligation each of us has to make our teammates better. In this book, Satch challenges us to be accountable, humble, grateful and the best teammates we can be in life. He connects the crucial dots between our attitude and actions off the court and our ability to succeed on it. He reminds us that, while winning is a worthy aspiration, playing the game and living the right way is much more important and impactful.

Winning with Purpose is an inspirational, empowering read that offers practical principles which, if applied, will lift your game and life to a championship level!

Clark Kellogg, 2013

A SPECIAL MESSAGE FROM DICK VITALE

In the game of life, just like in sports, motivation is a key ingredient to becoming a winner. If you're not inspired, it's tough to succeed.

Satch Sullinger is a master motivator, and the principles he has used to inspire and improve the lives of countless kids, including his three sons, are on powerful display in *Winning with Purpose*. Satch stands for family, building character and doing things the right way on and off the court, and his approach to getting better at the game of life and becoming the best teammates we can be represents everything I believe in.

Satch was honored as the 2010 Naismith National High School Basketball Coach of the Year, so his resume speaks for itself. He is the father of Jared Sullinger, a member of the Boston Celtics and the former Diaper Dandy of the Year at Ohio State.

We all know, and I've said it many times, that life is simple: If you make the right decisions, good things will happen for you. If you make the wrong ones, you'll be stuck in a negative world. This book provides a strong foundation for sound decision-making and bringing our best to the game each day, including great attitude and effort, understanding and accepting accountability, trusting our teammates and refusing to make excuses.

Satch Sullinger is a championship coach and a winner in the game of life, and the principles he explores here will help you succeed, too, if you apply them.

Winning with Purpose is a winner for players and coaches, parents and kids everywhere! This book is awesome, baby, with a capital *A*!

—Dick Vitale, ESPN college basketball analyst

PART I

PART I

Introduction: Wins, Losses and Lessons

Winning with Purpose in life means putting individual goals aside and using the gifts God gives us to help make our teammates better, which, in turn, allows all of us to succeed. Playing only for ourselves is a losing proposition because even when we win, we come up short.

Greatness is not defined by talent alone. Rather, it is rooted in quality character and reflected in our lasting impact on others. We've all seen examples of talented players who became wrapped up in themselves and watched their careers and lives unravel because of it. No matter how many games they won or points they scored, their talent was ultimately buried beneath the rubble of questionable character.

To achieve greatness, we must give our best each day without asking for anything in return, trusting that our effort and intention will create the path to our potential. We'll make mistakes along the way, but if we learn from them and refuse to repeat them, we can't fail.

My hope is that this book will help you realize the success that is possible for all of us if we're living a life of purpose and our commitment to team is constant. Our determination to make the right choices, for the right reasons, no matter how inconvenient it may be for us at times, is the only way to build a strong foundation for sustained life success. We must build that foundation brick by brick … there are no shortcuts.

As a young man, I learned the hard way what happens when we look for shortcuts and, as you'll read, it almost cost me everything. That experience, though unpleasant, has proven priceless to me as a husband and father and teacher and coach — as a teammate — over the years. I've witnessed the power that using our skills to support others and pursuing success together brings, and there's nothing like it.

I have a background in basketball, with three sons who played in college, one who plays in the NBA, and a coaching resume that covers decades. Though I hung up my coaching whistle recently, I love and respect the game, and remain close to it. I'm grateful for the opportunity I enjoyed to learn from — and help mold the athletic talent, character and crucial life skills of — countless youngsters

Much of what I have to share here is steeped in the lessons I learned about discipline, desire, integrity and old-fashioned work ethic from mentors who were dear to me, including my Grandpa Jim and Pat Penn, my coach at Oberlin College.

Hopefully, you'll understand how those lessons have helped me in my life and career, and see how they can help you, too … if you'll commit to following them. Remember, there are no shortcuts.

Sharing with you the lessons I've learned is part of my journey to keep improving and, more importantly, help my teammates continue to get better. And we're all teammates in this world.

Tip-Off: We're All Teammates

As a teenager in the late '60s, I witnessed the powerful commitment to purpose inherent to the civil rights movement in America, and it made an unforgettable impression on me and helped form my belief in the ability each of us has to make a positive impact on others, no matter the challenges we may face along the way.

Watching the amazing efforts of John F. Kennedy, his brother Robert, Martin Luther King Jr. and Malcolm X, among many, to effect change despite deadly opposition made me realize what is possible for us if we'll put ego aside and focus on helping our teammates. No matter the labels we toss around in trying to separate ourselves from others, we're all teammates in this world and it's our duty to help lift the team to greatness, not tear it apart.

Though the paths these and other leaders took in advancing the cause of equal rights differed, the common ground they shared was a clear message of self-betterment and societal accountability. While we must realize that life has never been and will never be "fair" (it isn't supposed to be), it shouldn't stop us from filling our unique roles in an effort to make the team better. If we seek only solo glory, we lose—and so does the team.

Improving ourselves and lifting our teammates means letting go of the bitterness and bad energy we're carrying from the past. We can't undo what's been done. The only way we can make a positive difference is by maximizing the moment at hand. After all, *it's the only moment we can affect.* That doesn't mean we don't remember, of course. They say the past is a great predictor of future behavior, that if we fail to learn from our mistakes we're destined to repeat them. It's crucial we take the lessons there in our experiences, especially those painful ones, and grow from them and commit to doing better next time. But we'll never reach our potential as team members, and therefore can't help lift the team to its zenith, if we're dragging bitterness with us. If we're stewing about our lack of playing time in the last game or are upset about the official's call on our previous possession, we'll miss the key shot in crunch time and cost our team the game.

FIRST QUARTER

Early Adversity

Growing up, I faced adversity right out of the gate. My dad wasn't around much, didn't care to be, and my mom was in and out of relationships with other men. Our household was in flux. It seemed we were always on the move.

My dad played professional basketball before blacks were allowed in the NBA, before Jackie Robinson came along and broke down the color barriers in professional sports. My dad played with a traveling team called the Sioux City Colored Ghosts, an all-African-American club that started as a softball team and added basketball so they could compete year-round. Supposedly, the Colored Ghosts were the first team to beat the Harlem Globetrotters, in Kenton, Ohio, before the Boston Generals began traveling with the Globetrotters as their designated punch-line opposition.

All the Colored Ghost players had nicknames, like "String Bean" Potts and "Shorty" Buckner and "Tree" Collins. My dad's name was Harold, and he was a big man with a booming voice. He had huge hands, too. The other players on the team said his hands were so big they looked like suitcases dangling from his long arms.

So they called my dad "Suitcase." Suitcase Sullinger was a good player, considered by teammates to be the best passer and defender on the Colored Ghosts club.

Unfortunately, my dad was a player off the court, too. He refused to commit to being a full-time father and husband, and he didn't care much what was happening with my mom, Cheryl, or me. He was always somewhere else, with this woman or that. He showed up one day with one of his girlfriends and told my mom she could learn some things from the woman about how to satisfy a man. My mom left him for good that day, with me in tow. That was the start of us bouncing from place to place.

My mom, my half-brother Larry (he was seven years older than I, a product of my mom's relationship with a man named Leslie Abney) and I lived for a while in a dingy, crowded rooming house in Columbus, Ohio. We shared a tiny bathroom with a bunch of strangers. Despite our troubles, I knew my mom loved me. I never felt love from my dad. He'd visit us on weekends sometimes, but eventually stopped coming. His absence in my life took a big emotional toll on me, one I would only later begin to grasp. No matter how little he seemed to care about us, though, I still yearned for his presence.

One time in particular during those years sums up my struggle to deal with his absence. It was a beautiful spring morning, and I was about seven. My mom had remarried and we were living with my stepdad and his kids. I was lying in bed and heard the birds chirping outside. My mom and stepdad and his kids were laughing and joking around in another room. It sounded like they were having so much fun together, but I couldn't bring myself to join them. I refused to let my guard down. My stepdad had tried to make me feel like a part of the family, but it didn't work. I felt like I didn't belong. He was a good man but he wasn't my dad, and I couldn't fake it. There was no emotional connection between us. He'd get angry whenever my mom or I spoke of my dad. My mom didn't want to upset him, so she discouraged me from talking about my dad. I kept all those feelings bottled up inside, and they would later boil over in ugly fashion. I felt alone and out of place.

I decided then that if I were lucky enough to be a father someday, I would be there to raise my children, no matter what. I'd do whatever it took to make them feel secure, to let them know I loved them, to make sure they'd never feel the emptiness I felt that spring morning.

Steadying Influence

When I was 12, my mom sent me to live with my Grandma Nanny and Grandpa Jim. My mom claimed it was because Grandpa Jim worked nights and someone needed to be there to look after Grandma Nanny. Larry had been staying with them, but joined the Army and left. His departure provided a timely excuse for my mom and stepdad, who had decided I didn't fit in with their "new" family and seized the opportunity to send me elsewhere.

Grandma Nanny was a freckle-faced Irish woman, kind and spirited. Jim was my step-grandfather, but we connected instantly. He would become a father figure and positive influence for me. Grandpa Jim was a hard-working man, rough around the edges and formally uneducated. But he was one of the smartest men I've ever known. He was strong in character and a keen reader of people. He was matter-of-fact about right and wrong. "You can't defend wrong," he'd say, "so do the right thing. Then you won't be stuck trying to justify a bad decision later."

Grandpa Jim spoke of trusting one's self, no matter the opinions of others. "You'll have to die your own death," he'd say, "so you might as well live your own life." He meant that we're all accountable for our own circumstances, our own situation in life, so why leave our destiny up to others? It's our job to make it happen. In the end, he'd say, we either get the job done or we don't. All our talk and intentions fall away. It's about finishing the job. Grandpa Jim worked as a cook at Max's Steakhouse in downtown Columbus. On bustling Saturday nights, he'd get home in the wee hours of the morning, his arms full of leftover cakes and pies. I loved waiting up with Grandma Nanny for him to arrive, excited for the goodies I knew he'd bring. Grandpa Jim liked his booze, and he always brought a bottle of something or other to share with Grandma Nanny. We'd sit 'til dawn, the three of us, talking and laughing and carrying on. Then, Grandma Nanny would fry up a mess of fish and potatoes. We'd eat 'til we were stuffed and fall off to sleep.

Grandpa Jim didn't work on Sundays, so we'd spend the whole day together. He'd take me to the movies over at Livingston Theatre or out for a slice of pizza. In the fall, we'd watch our beloved Cleveland Browns play on television. He brought stability to my life at a crucial time. I believe everything happens for a reason in life and, though I was oblivious to it then, being sent to live with Grandpa Jim was God's work.

While my bond with Grandpa Jim meant the world to me, it wasn't a cure-all for the deeply-rooted feelings of rejection and abandonment I was carrying due to my dad's absence in my life and my mom sending me elsewhere to live because she and my stepdad didn't want me around. I felt like I didn't truly belong *anywhere*. Those toxic feelings boiled inside me for too long and I kept them bottled up.

My physical size only added to my sense of isolation. I was always much bigger than other kids my age and it caused problems for me. At 13, I was already 6'4", and weighed 225 lbs. For some reason, people seemed threatened by my size. Not just my classmates but their parents, too. When I'd show up at the other kids' houses to hang out, their parents looked at me like I was some kind of freak, like they didn't want me to be around their kids. Because I was so big for my age, I became an easy target to other kids. They taunted me, pushed me, but I refused to fight back. They called me "Baby Huey," a cutting reference to the oversized, naïve cartoon figure from the fifties.

Keeping my emotions locked inside began to take a physical toll on me. My hair started to fall out, which the doctors attributed to my constant state of anxiety. It fell out in patches and, oddly, when it grew back, it was blonde in color. Kids at school called me "Apache" because of the blonde patches in my hair, and made mock Indian war call sounds when they saw me in the hallway. Finally, I'd had enough, and the angst I felt boiled over in a bad way.

I became aggressive and began to use my size as a weapon. I pummeled my tormentors, seeking to pay them back for the emotional harm they'd inflicted. I sought physical confrontation whenever possible and started to enjoy the false sense of power that violence provided. Beating up on other kids made me somehow feel like I finally fit in, like I was finally "one of the guys." That illusion of being in control crept into my mindset and would cost me plenty later on.

My family was a potpourri of step-parents and half-brothers and half-sisters and numerous aunts and uncles, from my mom and dad's multiple relationships and marriages. It seemed I was always trying to adjust. But one thing never changed: From that difficult spring morning at my stepdad's house, I was determined things would be different for my kids when I became a father. I'd do whatever it took to surround them with a loving and stable home environment. Thankfully, that's what my wife Barbara and I were able to give to my sons, J.J., Julian and Jared, while they grew up. And I never took it for granted. I still try to let Barb and my boys know daily how much they mean to me. It drives them crazy sometimes, but I always want them to know.

I met Barb in college at Oberlin University and she was a game-changer for me. I had graduated from South High School in

Columbus in 1967, had been a role player on the basketball team but was a star in my mind. I was aggressive and arrogant, and it led to dark days for me after high school. I thought I was the exception to the rule and wasn't concerned about the consequences of my actions.

Shortcuts to Dead Ends

After graduation, I pushed aside the idea of attending college. I was self-absorbed, my ego blocking commitment to my potential. I was drafted into the Army and, in hindsight, the discipline I'd have received there would have been the best thing for me at the time. But I was deferred from duty because of a steel pin that had been surgically inserted in my hip to combat degeneration when I was younger. I was still living with Grandpa Jim and Grandma Nanny, and I found myself with lots of free time on my hands.

I started running the streets and got caught up in the "action" out there. Whenever one party ended, it seemed another was just beginning. Gradually, the shady characters I met there became replacement role models for me, so-called "friends" who welcomed me and made me feel important and claimed they had my back, no matter what. Those hazy days spent raising hell quickly turned to years. I jumped from job to job, never making what I felt was any "real" money. I complained that I deserved a better opportunity but hadn't done the work necessary to put myself in position for it. My attitude and effort were poor. So I decided to take a shortcut.

I began to sell drugs, including cocaine and heroin, cruising the streets with dirty money and the fancy car and tailor-made clothes it provided. I used drugs, too, staying high on my supply. I was sharp-dressed but I was a world away from comfortable. I carried a gun. When you're selling drugs, you're always on edge because your "customers" are mostly junkies who'd do anything, even kill you, to get your stash. Drug dealers see everyone as a potential dollar sign, a possible customer. Even kids. Drug dealers don't care how young their customers are. The parents of those kids you're pushing drugs to want to hurt you, also, because of the damage you're causing to their families.

In that filthy marketplace, your "competitors," your fellow dealers, want to wipe you out so that they can steal your customers. When you're selling drugs, it's the kind of company you keep. You become isolated. You stop spending time with family and friends, people who truly care about you, because you're ashamed of how you're living and afraid they'll get tangled up in your twisted web. To top it off, you're constantly trying to stay a step ahead of the police, peeking around corners, casting a wary eye at anyone you meet. But you can't run forever. Sooner or later, the law finds you. Karma finds you.

Ironically, during the time I was selling drugs, I had a job with the Ohio Youth Commission counseling troubled kids, many of whom were fighting to overcome substance-abuse issues that dealers like me had helped to create. I was living a double life, warning kids about the evils of drugs while I was pushing dope and getting high. I was living a lie. It may sound strange, but I wanted the best for those youngsters. Despite my own struggles, I saw myself in those kids and knew if they could straighten themselves out and avoid taking shortcuts, they could go on to live productive lives. I was lost to darkness but I never lost faith. Even at my lowest point, I believed God had good things in store for me. I had no idea how His plan would unfold.

When police smashed through the door of my house one night and found me in a pile of drugs and money, I was confronted with brutal reality. It proved a point of no return for me.

I faced a long prison sentence and I was scared. The police tried to get me to give up information about my drug suppliers, telling me I could make things easier for myself. But I refused.

I knew if I told the cops anything, I'd end up dead. I felt sick in my soul for a long time about the way I'd been living, knowing that what I was doing was causing pain to others and that my actions were the opposite of what I really believed in my heart. I knew I was on a dead-end road to prison or death. Now, life in prison seemed certain. All I could do was pray and ask God for a second chance to live with purpose and make a positive difference.

Second Chances

Pat Penn, a longtime high school coach in Columbus and the coach at Oberlin College at the time, knew me from my playing days at South High (I made the game-clinching free throws in a battle with his Bishop Ready team). Coach Penn had always gone out of his way to talk with me, to get to know me, to let me know he believed I could make something special of my life. He had become a sort of father figure to me, since my dad wasn't around. When Coach Penn heard of my legal troubles, he rushed to my side. He appeared at my court hearing and insisted on speaking with the judge about me. It would have been easy for Coach Penn to write me off when he got word of my wrongdoings. Instead, he was there for me when I needed it most. He told the judge that he believed in me, in my character, saying that despite my bad decision to become involved with drugs, he was convinced of my potential and that I'd learn from my terrible mistakes if given a second chance.

The judge decided not to send me to prison, sentencing me instead to probation with education-focused terms. He said if I'd commit myself to trying to go to college, to toeing the line and following the rules and staying out of trouble, I could avoid prison. He said there was no margin for error and that if I messed up again and got into trouble, I'd be locked up for a long time. He said he'd evaluate my progress regularly and that, if I proved myself, he'd expunge my arrest record. I was thankful beyond belief. I knew I'd nearly ruined my life, had come so close to throwing away my future. I was grateful for the second chance I'd been given and was committed to making a positive difference.

I never touched drugs or alcohol again. I studied for the SAT college entrance exam and dusted off my basketball skills, which had been shelved since high school. I scored well enough on the test and, at Coach Penn's urging, enrolled at Oberlin, a small liberal arts college in northeast Ohio. I was a freshman in college at age 26. Coach Penn welcomed me, making a spot on his team available for me if I'd prove myself and make the most of my opportunity. I arrived at Oberlin in 1975 with plenty of street smarts but lots to learn. The feeling of control I'd had, of calling the shots while running the streets in Columbus, was gone, replaced by the anxiety of being a no-name in an unfamiliar place — and a 26-year-old no-name at that. I felt like I didn't belong again, like I didn't fit in with the other students. Being older was part of it, but so were my recent legal troubles.

Part of establishing my identity at Oberlin and getting a new start meant unloading a secret burden I'd been carrying since I was a kid. Though Sullinger was my real last name, my stepdad had enrolled me in school for years using the name of James Adams. James was my real first name, but Adams was my stepdad's last name. He never told me why he did it, but I figured it was his way of trying to create more distance between my real father and me. And I just accepted it. My stepdad hadn't gone through any official legal process to change my last name to Adams, but that's the name he used when he enrolled me in school. For years, people knew me as James Adams and I never told them otherwise.

When I got to college, however, I was compelled to come clean, to myself and everyone else, to reclaim my original name and build a new life as James Sullinger. So that's what I did.

I met Barbara my first day on campus at Oberlin. I was walking in the dormitory hallway when I saw her, and I offered some weak one-liner, a feeble attempt at humor, feigning bravado. We began talking and I was struck immediately by her kindness. She was a 21-year-old senior and I was a raw, 26-year-old freshman, but we connected instantly. She saw right through my tough outer shell, saw my fragility and insecurity. She made me feel like I was worth something. We became friends, and eventually, we started dating.

From the beginning, she brought out the best in me. Barbara was no-nonsense, tough like me but polished and well-rounded. She was raised in New York City, came from an educated, well-to-do family. Her father was vice president of a large bank and her mother was an education consultant to Mayor Dinkins. Ours was a classic "opposites attract" kind of relationship, me from a bare-bones, unsettled upbringing and her from a solid, well-to-do one.

Barbara's friends at Oberlin came from upper-crust families and they tried to discourage her from dating me, telling her I wasn't good enough for her, that I was little more than a street thug. But Barbara wasn't fazed by where I came from or my recent troubles. She stayed by my side. She helped me through those growing pains at Oberlin that came with understanding what accountability meant, with learning how to change my ways and become a better person and to live with purpose. Ironically, many of those friends of hers who had tried to keep us apart have long since been married, gotten divorced, and had all kinds of marital problems. Barbara has always been there to share ideas and see me through my peaks and valleys. She's set me straight more times than I can remember. She is my best friend and a wonderful mother to our sons.

While I wish I had never gotten involved with drugs, those painful lessons have proven helpful to me in working with kids over the years, whether players on my teams or students in my classroom or youngsters in the neighborhoods, who may be tempted to take shortcuts like I did. Kids see the drug dealers with their fancy cars, the money, the bling, and can be sucked in by it. It looks like an easy way out, but it only leads to bad places. When I talk with kids facing those temptations, I feel a genuine connection with them that comes from having been there, from having seen the overdoses and shootings and been at the funerals of friends. The kids I talk with seem to feel that connection, too. They know they can trust me. They're able to lower their emotional guard with me and understand that shortcuts are really just dead-ends.

Like Grandpa Jim said, when it comes to decision-making, it's simple: "You can't defend wrong!" Unfortunately, despite his warnings, I learned that lesson the hard way. His words still ring in my ears. He believed we all know what the right choice is for us in the moment, that we can "feel" when we're about to make our decision whether our choice will impact us and others positively and ultimately lead to growth or destruction. He said we know what the right decisions are, so trying to defend the wrong one after the damage is done is useless. Make the right decision because we can't defend wrong.

Learning from Mistakes

We all make mistakes in life and none of us is perfect. Sometimes, we make the wrong decisions. When we do, however, the way we respond to the fallout determines where we're headed.

The ability to learn from our mistakes is a key component of good character, and our commitment to making the most of a second chance says much about our makeup. Some treat second chances as a "get over," an opening to keep deceiving others, to feign remorse for the aftermath of their actions while continuing to live selfishly, without care for the impact of their decisions on others, especially their teammates.

These people refuse ownership of their mistakes and aren't motivated to make better choices. Instead, they waste energy and time "milking the system," sidestepping responsibility and blaming others for their bad decisions. To them, it's never their fault. They repeat their mistakes, expecting someone will always be there to bail them out. They get better at bluffing and refuse to improve. When the heat for their poor choices relents, they resume their reckless ways until trouble brews again. They keep serving the same old irresponsible soup ... they just serve it in a different bowl each time.

Others, however, savor their second chances and strive to get better. They acknowledge their missteps and the impact of their actions on teammates. They find the lessons in their mistakes and are determined not to repeat them. Their hearts are right and their conscience is clear. They understand accountability means making the right decisions for the right reasons, consistently.

Mistakes are part of the game for all of us, but I believe if our intention is right, is truly about the team's best interests, then even when we stumble, we'll bounce back better from it and our teammates will, too. We'll pick up on those subtle signs God places in our path. I believe that's what fate is. It's God's way of guiding us while staying anonymous.

If our decisions stem from selfishness, however, from trying to tear down teammates to make ourselves look better, our bad intent will boomerang back to us. Karma will settle the score and we'll be on the short end of it.

Coach Penn's Character Test

My growing pains at Oberlin began and ended with Coach Penn. He had helped me get another chance in life and made it clear when I arrived at Oberlin that my effort and attitude would determine whether I sank or swam. But the opportunity to redefine myself was there for the taking if I were willing to put in the work.

Coach Penn was an old-school disciplinarian who challenged me from the start. When it came to doing things the right way, Coach Penn never sugarcoated anything and wouldn't allow excuses to get in the way of growth, as a person or a player or a team. He likened excuses to bushes that people hide behind to avoid the hard work of improvement. Hide behind that bush, that excuse, he'd say, while potential passes you by. Coach Penn was skilled at chopping away those bushes, at erasing hiding places for players and forcing them to face responsibility. He refused to accept anything but a player's best effort. His straightforward approach was strikingly similar to Grandpa Jim's.

Coach Penn believed talk was useless if not accompanied by action. He walked his talk and expected the same from his players. Early in my freshman season at Oberlin, Coach Penn was relentless in his scrutiny of me during practice, and was noticeably harder on me than on my teammates. He screamed at me, singled me out and showed frustration with me in front of the team when I made even the smallest mistakes. I didn't understand it at the time, but he was testing my character, my mettle, and wanted to see how I'd respond to his elimination of those "excuse bushes" he talked about. I was convinced he'd brought me to Oberlin to be The Man, the star-in-the-making player who would lead the team to glory. *Just leave me alone*, I thought, and *I'll show you and the team how it's done.* But he didn't ease up on me. I was angry and confused.

During practice one day, my ego boiled over. When Coach Penn screamed at me for a mistake I'd made, I stormed out of practice. *To hell with this*, I thought. *I'll go back home to Columbus. I'll enroll at Capital University and play for Vince Chickerella*, a great coach who had tried to recruit me. *I'll be The Man on campus at Capital, and I'll do things my way.*

I returned to my dorm room to plan my move. Within a few minutes, there was a knock at my door. It was Coach Penn. He knew I was frustrated and anticipated my intent. "Where's your suitcase?" he asked. "I'll help you pack." I was stunned. "If you're this damned soft," he said, "I don't want you to play for me. Go back to Columbus and run the streets again or play ball somewhere else if you want. If you decide to play at another school, please let me know so I can schedule a game against your team because, as undisciplined as you are, if you're our opponent, it should be an easy win for us."

He was challenging me to grow up. There were no more bushes left for me to hide behind. It was a breaking point for me. Either I'd run back to Columbus and away from accountability, or I'd stay, check my ego and do what it took to improve as a person and player. I was silent for a few moments. "I'm not going anywhere!" I exclaimed. "I'll prove to you what I'm made of."

Coach Penn didn't blink. "When I yell at you in practice," he continued, "it's because I expect good things from you and I see your potential as a leader. Not just in basketball, but in life. It's when I *stop* yelling at you, *stop* pushing you to give your best, that you should be concerned, because that would mean I've given up on you, that I don't think you're worth the effort anymore."

His words lit a fire in my soul. At practice the next day, I played like a man possessed. I played the same way the next practice and the one after that. I was determined to play so well that Coach Penn would struggle to find a mistake I'd made. I played with passion and focus and good things began to happen for our team. We reeled off sixteen wins in a row, captured the Ohio Athletic Conference championship, made the national postseason tournament and advanced to the regional finals. We enjoyed the most successful season in Oberlin basketball history at the time. It was a total team effort, with everybody filling their roles, each player using their skills to support their teammates.

Our success was extra special to me because I had finally begun to tap that potential Coach Penn talked about.

The accountability light had come on for me. I'd seen the power accepting ownership of our actions with no excuses brings, on and off the court, and had begun to embrace it. Everything Coach Penn preached to his players about accountability, about handling our business off the court so it could feed our success on the court, about learning to be a part of something bigger than ourselves ... it wasn't just words to me anymore.

You Play the Game the Way You Live Your Life

The bottom line to the lessons I learned from Coach Penn is this: *You play the game the way you live your life.* It's my guiding philosophy and I've emphasized it countless times to my players over the years. It means our performance on the court, especially when crunch time comes, mirrors how we're handling our business *away* from the court. If we're working hard in the classroom, for example, are treating ourselves and others with respect, are seeking to *solve* instead of looking to *complain*, are filling our family and societal roles effectively, we'll carry that confidence and good karma with us to the court and will put ourselves in position to succeed when crunch time comes. But if we're living selfishly, recklessly, avoiding responsibility and blaming others, that negative karma will prevent us from coming through in the clutch. *You play the game the way you live your life.* We can't separate the two.

Through Coach Penn's lessons, I began to see the powerful impact living with purpose could make and started to experience the positive results that come from accepting accountability. He was a championship-caliber coach, but Pat Penn's most important lessons had little to do with basketball. He taught us about *life*, about how to rise during crunch time of the biggest game there is.

Coach Penn looked beyond the "player" part of a kid, beyond the physical skills that are easy to see. He cared about the mental and emotional pieces of kids, too, those parts that, if nourished, could help them reach their potential as *people*, not just athletes. Coach Penn was about developing all three pieces equally: the physical, mental and emotional that, when added together, equal One, the complete player, the *whole person*.

I became passionate about spreading Coach Penn's message of living with purpose to others, especially kids. I believed I could utilize the lessons I'd learned from my own mistakes, from trying to take shortcuts, to help kids avoid similar pitfalls. If I could get to kids early enough, I thought, maybe they wouldn't have to learn the hard way like I did. I could help them learn to believe in themselves, perhaps to understand the power of living with purpose. I was named captain of the basketball team during my junior and senior seasons at Oberlin and, thanks to the impact Pat Penn had made on my life, decided I wanted to become a coach, too.

Digger's Early Influence and Lasting Impression

After deciding that coaching was my calling, I began paying close attention to numerous successful coaches and the variety of strategic styles their teams employed on the court. From a defensive coaching perspective, Digger Phelps, the longtime Notre Dame coach and ESPN college basketball analyst, was the first to open my eyes to what was possible.

Digger was the first coach I saw who switched up defenses continuously when an opponent had the ball. He didn't just stick with the same old defense the whole game. His teams thrived on changing it up during an opponent's possession, from one defense to the next, based on where the ball was on the court, in an effort to disrupt the other team's offensive flow. Digger inspired me to explore various defensive approaches, and consistent relentless defensive changeups to control the tempo of a game became a hallmark of our most successful teams at Northland High later in my career.

When our teams scored a transition basket, for example, we'd jump into a press, then fall back into man-to-man. If our opponent was bringing the ball full court following a dead-ball situation, our defense would apply run-and-jump pressure at half-court. After a successful free-throw attempt by our team, we'd jump into a 1-2-2 zone. If we missed the free throw, our defenders followed the opponent's first pass to the sideline or baseline in traffic.

With Coach Penn at Oberlin, our teams had always been anchored to a 1-3-1 zone approach on defense. Coach Penn believed strongly in zone defense, so that's what we played. Zone defense was all I knew. When it worked for us, it worked, but unfortunately, when teams solved our zone defense, we had nothing else to throw at them.

With constant transition from pressing to man-to-man to zone defense, Digger's teams confused their opponents and controlled the tempo of the game. He made me realize that defense is the key. He inspired me to understand the importance of being fundamentally sound on defense and how to execute effective man-to-man defense. Understanding how strong defense worked helped me to become a better offensive coach, too, because I was able to anticipate how those strong defenses would react.

SECOND QUARTER

Out of Nowhere

My father was there the day I graduated from Oberlin. I was shocked to see him in the crowd. *Why now?* I thought. After all these years and everything that's happened ... He had cast aside my mom and me, had ignored his responsibilities as a father and husband so he could run off with his girlfriends and do as he pleased without concern for the consequences. Now, here he was. Just like that. Emotion swept over me. When we spoke, he was indifferent, as if his lifetime absence had somehow been trivial, as if he'd simply pushed a fast-forward button on holding himself accountable for his choices and decided now was the time to jump in. I knew he was proud I'd made it through college; he probably didn't think I'd make it there anyway. He told me he was pleased that it seemed my troubles were in the past and that I'd begun to make the most of my second chance in life.

It was a powerful moment for us. When he started to talk about his mistakes, however, I stopped him. I didn't care to hear his excuses for not being there. *If he'd cared enough about us*, I thought, *he'd have been there.* But my yearning for a connection with him, my search for that stamp of approval only a father can provide, was still strong. Despite my bitterness toward him, that crack of emotional daylight in me remained.

The power to forgive can make or break our lives. It was hard for me to do, but I decided that day to forgive my father and opened my mind and heart to the idea of a new relationship with him. Any discussion about the past, however, was off-limits for a while. I had to take our new relationship a small step at a time.

I graduated from Oberlin with a degree in education and took a job as an assistant to Coach Penn for two seasons, continuing to soak up his knowledge of life and basketball. It was a great experience for me and further fueled my belief in the power coaches have to impact lives. I left Oberlin to attend Grambling State University in Louisiana, where I was a graduate assistant coach and earned a master's degree in athletic administration.

USA Basketball and a Special Young Man

In 1982, I became the first fulltime black administrator for the U.S. Olympic basketball program, later known as USA Basketball, in Colorado Springs. I was the first full-time black administrator for any of the Olympic sports. The job afforded me the opportunity to learn from Bill Wall, the longtime executive director of USA Basketball, and to head our organization's efforts at the U.S. Olympic Festival in Indianapolis that summer, which became a landmark event. Olympic Festivals don't exist anymore, but they were big deals back then. Many of the individual sports federations used the festivals as pre-selection competitions for Olympic teams. My experience at the Olympic Festival was an eye-opener for many reasons, not all of them positive.

As administrator for the basketball program, I led a staff responsible for a myriad of duties for the men's and women's programs at the festival, including the coordination of games, practice facilities, interviews, entertainment, dining, etc. Though ours was a total team effort, the staff buck stopped with me for final decisions. From my arrival in Indy, however, it was apparent some were still struggling with the notion of a black man in a leadership role, and their indignation was overt.

While our staff awaited transportation from the airport to the hotel following our arrival in Indianapolis, a loudmouth attorney lingering nearby learned that I was the staff leader. He stared at me in wide-eyed disbelief and tossed a business card at me. *"You're* in charge? Here's my phone number in case you get arrested!" His inference was obvious.

In another instance, I reserved a table by phone for our staff at a nice restaurant upstairs at the old Market Square Arena so that we could dine with a view of the Festival games taking place below. I arrived at the restaurant before the others, and was about to take a seat at our table. As I started to sit, however, I was informed by the hostess that the table was reserved for basketball staff members only. I told her I was part of the staff and that I, myself, had made the reservation. She didn't believe me and insisted I leave the table. Just then, Bill Wall's daughter arrived and, sensing the tension, explained to the hostess that not only was I a member of the basketball staff but that I, in fact, was the leader of it. The hostess offered a weak apology and slunk away.

Despite those awkward incidents, the Olympic Festival was a tremendous experience for me overall. I'll always be grateful to Bill Wall for the opportunity he gave me to prove myself.

One of the highlights of the festival for me was meeting a special young man named Wayman Tisdale, then a freshman-to-be at Oklahoma who went on to become an Olympic gold medalist, three-time All-American and NBA star. Wayman hailed from Tulsa, was the son of a pastor, and had a smile and energy about him that lit up a room. Wayman and I enjoyed lunch together one afternoon and just clicked. We talked about many things, the least of which was basketball.

During our conversation, I was struck by Wayman's humility and awareness and appreciation for life, especially at such a young age, and it became apparent to me that he was headed for great things, on and off the court. Coincidentally, my son Jared won the first Wayman Tisdale Award as college basketball's top freshman player in 2011. It was an honor to hear Jared's name mentioned with Wayman's. At the ceremony, I recalled my long-ago conversation with Wayman and shared my special memory of it with Wayman's lovely wife, Regina. Wayman was an amazing person with enormous talent, and he defined class and courage and what living the right way means. Though he's gone, he remains a huge inspiration to many.

A Good One Gone and a Son Arrives

In the fall of '82, while living in Colorado Springs, I learned that Grandpa Jim had died. All the memories came flooding back and it was overwhelming to me. Those late nights spent talking and laughing and carrying on with him and my grandmother as a boy, those Sunday afternoons spent watching our favorite Cleveland Browns on television or going to the movies or out for pizza, the time we spent together hanging out like best buddies after I'd graduated from high school. He was the only one who called me "Jimmy," and was the only one who could get away with it. I returned to Columbus for his funeral. He wore a tie when he was buried that I'd bought him years before.

Grandpa Jim had taught me so much about respect and work ethic and staying true to myself, about the importance of doing the right things in life. He'd loved me when I needed it most. I would miss him terribly. I still hear his voice guiding me and will always stay true to what I learned from him. Shortly after his death, our first child, James Jr., or "J.J.," was born. Facing the prospect of constant travel and time away from Barbara and our newborn son in my duties with USA Basketball, I left the job behind and we moved to Columbus. I had promised myself as a boy that if I were lucky enough to be a father someday, I'd be there for my child throughout, and I intended to fulfill that promise. To me, it was special to be doing it back home in Columbus.

I got a job as a substitute teacher for a while, and landed my first head coaching job at East High School. East had won plenty of games prior to my arrival, but was a place where poor character was prevalent. We had a long way to go to turn the program around, and I believed it could only happen if we established a foundation of strong character, of purpose and passion. We could begin to win the right way only when we trusted each other, when we believed in sacrificing personal glory to become a part of something bigger than ourselves.

Establishing a foundation of character for the program meant eliminating those bushes Coach Penn talked about, those excuses players hide behind to avoid the hard work of improvement.

So I began to root out the bushes. I've always believed that, as a coach, you win with character. Talent does not always equal quality character; in many cases, far from it. Too often, we see examples of talented athletes who find themselves in trouble due to poor character. A team may be full of talented players but if those players lack quality character, that team will fall short when it matters most. The team may win a bunch of games, but it won't win the "banner games," the biggest games, because somewhere along the way, during crunch time of those big games, that lack of character, that "gotta get mine!" attitude by a player will rear its ugly head.

It goes back to playing the game the way we live our lives, to holding ourselves accountable away from the court and handling our schoolwork or job or family situation to the best of our ability, consistently. If a player won't make the necessary effort to handle their obligations off the court, that player, no matter how talented, cannot be counted upon when crunch time comes on the court. It's called karma. If we're cheating ourselves and our teammates over *there*, it's only a matter of time until it shows up over here, too.

Making Words Matter

My efforts to eliminate those "excuse bushes" that players hide behind, including the biggest one called *ego*, introduced a defining challenge for me as head coach at East High. We were about to depart for a road game, and all of our players had arrived on time to board the team bus for the trip except one. Our best player showed up late, nonchalant, and attempted to board the bus. I had been preaching sacrifice and selflessness in the name of team success, and now our best player had shown up late without reason. The other players watched to see how I'd respond. It was put up or shut up time for me. If I truly believed what I'd been preaching to my players, my decision was obvious.

I refused to allow our star player to board the bus and we departed. The player found his own ride to the game, a hundred-mile trip, and insisted he be allowed to play. I again refused. He was furious. The star player and the rest of our team realized then that accountability was about action, not just words. I was determined to stand for the ideals I wanted our program to represent, that being a part of our team meant buying in to something bigger than any of us individually.

I was forced to "walk my talk." If a player were unable or unwilling to be where they were expected to be at a certain time, that player couldn't be counted on when crunch time came. Each of us was accountable to the team, including our best player. That incident pulled our players closer together. We lost the game that night but won our next thirteen games in a row. Our star player was never late again.

Winning Games, Losing Principal

To some, however, talent trumps all, and to hell with doing things the right way. For them, winning is all that matters, and character is trampled in a dirty dash to proclaim empty excellence. I was about to learn it the hard way as coach at East High and beyond, and it was an awakening for me.

We had begun to build a program of sound character at East, were winning plenty of games and doing it the right way. The future looked promising for us. In building a program, situations inevitably arise which threaten a character-first foundation, like the one where our star player showed up late to the team bus. When these situations occur, coaches can't afford to compromise. The definition of what the program represents must be clear. Otherwise, it's just talk. Like the old saying goes, "stand for something, or you'll fall for anything."

While at East, I dismissed from the team a talented player who'd failed in multiple ways to hold himself accountable, with issues in the classroom, on the court and in the community. Dismissing a player is always tough for a coach, but this player's poor behavior had become an obvious distraction to the team. When the school principal heard I'd kicked a good player off the team who could help us win games, he insisted I let the player rejoin the team.

The problems the player had caused were well-documented, but the principal didn't care. He had gotten a taste of what winning games was like as the program had steadily turned around, and accountability and integrity became afterthoughts to him. The principal at East wanted that player to play because he knew it would help us win more games, no matter the player's negative impact on the team. Grudgingly, I allowed the player back on the team. But I gave him very little playing time.

The principal was incensed at my actions. He charged me with insubordination and issued an ultimatum: resign or be fired. I've always felt, that for any relationship to thrive, including employer/employee, three things must be in place: First, we must be able to *understand our teammates*, understand the environment we're in and the conditions that affect the relationship. Second, we must feel that our teammates or coaches or bosses *understand us*, understand our approach and commitment to the job. Third, we must feel that we're *wanted*, that our teammates or coaches or bosses value our efforts to help the team succeed. It was obvious to me by his ultimatum that the principal no longer wanted me as coach at East, so I resigned.

Despite my resignation, I was named District Coach of the Year. To me, that award spoke to the values we had begun to instill in the program at East, to those players who had decided to hold themselves accountable, who had chosen selflessness and sacrifice in the name of team betterment. Those players realized that becoming a part of something bigger than any of them individually is where real glory is found. My Coach of the Year award was all about them and their commitment to purpose.

Later, it was discovered that the principal at East had illegally altered course grades for players to ensure their eligibility, and he was fired. Sadly, I wasn't surprised when I heard what he'd done.

Newborn Program, No Chance to Grow

I accepted a job as head coach at Franklin University in Columbus, a community college with a fledgling basketball program. I saw it as an exciting opportunity to help build something positive for the university and the community, a way to help the university lay a foundation for long-term athletic success. A key factor in my decision to take the job was commitment by the president of the university to back the program and to provide all possible resources in helping the program grow. Shortly after I accepted the job, however, he died suddenly and the situation changed dramatically.

The acting university president made it painfully clear that, not only was a new basketball program unimportant to him, but there would be little, if any, financial support for it. Indeed, our basketball program "budget" reflected his indifference. The budget wasn't sufficient to cover the most basic expenses, including hiring game officials, travel, etc. Though I wanted to make the situation work for our players, the outlook for the program quickly grew bleak. I searched for ways to cut costs. Instead of paying a driver, I drove the battered van assigned to us for travel to road games myself. Some of our trips required several hours of travel each way in dicey winter weather, and money in our budget for team lodging was non-existent.

The struggles with a complete lack of program support affected my focus on coaching and our players' ability to perform. The team had little talent or depth to begin with, a challenge inherent to most startup programs. In the best of circumstances, our team had no margin for error if we hoped to win. We lost thirteen of our first fourteen games, and it was all the ammunition the acting president needed to eliminate a program he cared nothing about. In a bizarre move, he declared that Franklin University would not be permitted to play games the following season against teams who'd beaten us by ten points or more during the current season. His edict was comical. I suggested to him that, given his parameters, our schedule the following season would likely be empty, because there wasn't a team around at the time that couldn't have beaten us by at least ten points.

It was obvious he intended to eliminate the basketball program. I met with him and didn't mince words. I suggested that if he and other administrators at Franklin wanted to kill the program, perhaps we should save everybody the time and trouble and do it immediately. After all, it wasn't fair to our players, or me, to commit to a program at a place that didn't support it. The acting president agreed, and the basketball program at Franklin University was ended before it had ever really begun.

That experience was a bitter pill to swallow for me, most importantly because it negatively impacted the players, who had given their all to try to get the program off the ground. But without support from the university, the situation was impossible. While I would obviously have preferred to avoid such ugly circumstances at Franklin, I gained valuable perspective from my experience there. It forced me to look inward, to examine whether I had somehow misread the situation or had expected more than others could give.

I spoke with fellow coaches whose opinions I trusted, coaches I knew wouldn't sugarcoat their opinions about the situation. I asked Barbara's opinion, too, because I knew she would give it to me straight. I concluded that I hadn't missed anything, and knew that my heart had been right and my intentions for the program at Franklin had been pure. I knew that if the president who had hired me, who had been excited about a new program's possibilities and pledged his support for it, hadn't died, things would've been much different. Our program at Franklin would have been given a chance to grow. I realized that no matter how passionate our players or I were about the program, it simply couldn't survive without university support. I chalked it up as one of those character-building situations that is tough to figure out at the time but makes us better down the road.

In my experiences as coach at East High and Franklin University, I'd received a quick education from opposite ends of the spectrum where core values and commitment to a program were concerned. At East, I'd seen a principal bent on doing whatever it took, in the worst way possible, to help the team win. That recklessness would cost him his job. At Franklin University, I witnessed an acting president's apathy for a new program, his complete disinterest in the program's existence at all, let alone winning or losing.

Each of those experiences cemented my belief in core values like trust and purpose. I believed it crucial to stick to the principles of good character I'd learned from Grandpa Jim and

Coach Pat Penn. I was convinced it was possible to build a winning program on a foundation of quality character. I had to look no further for affirmation of that belief than my days with Coach Penn at Oberlin.

My Brother 'Brief'

Though my father's absence in my life had taken an emotional toll, a silver lining in that dark cloud appeared for me in the form of my half-brother and eventual best friend, Harold Jr., nicknamed "Brief," for briefcase. My dad's nickname had been Suitcase, I'd been dubbed "Satchel," or Satch, and Brief carried on our Sullinger luggage nickname lineage. Silly nicknames, perhaps, but they stuck. Like I said, my dad had lived recklessly for most of his life and did as he pleased regardless of the consequences. He and my stepmom, Betty, had Brief together, and my dad was off and running again. Thanks to the efforts of "Mom Betty," as I called her, Brief and I got to know each other and became close. In the summers, I'd stay with Mom Betty and Brief for a few weeks. She wanted Brief to have a relationship with his older brother, his only brother. Those days spent with Brief and Mom Betty meant a lot to me. I felt special, with a little brother to look out for.

Mom Betty had family who lived in New Jersey, and she and Brief eventually moved to Camden. She was a teacher, and Brief became an All-American basketball player at Woodrow Wilson High. He was 6' 8", long and lean, could handle the ball and was a great shooter. He was ahead of his time as a post player, with his ability to do it all. Brief's coach at Woodrow Wilson High was Gary Williams, who became one of the all-time winning college coaches and led Maryland to the 2002 national championship. Coach Williams once said his first recruiting triumph was convincing Brief to come to Woodrow Wilson instead of tradition-rich rival Camden High.

Brief led Woodrow Wilson to an undefeated season and the state championship as a senior. He played two seasons for Coach Dick Schulz at Iowa. Coach Schulz later became executive director of the NCAA and head of the U.S. Olympic Committee. Brief dropped out of Iowa to join the Marine Corps, where he became a demolitions expert. Later, he returned to Columbus and his impact on my family would prove immense.

Instant Comfort Zone

Our sons were immersed in basketball from an early age, beginning with our eldest, J.J. They became fascinated with basketball. That fascination stemmed partly from my being a coach, of course, and their up-close exposure to the sport, but also because they grew up in the lap of great basketball tradition at The Ohio State University.

The names of Buckeye basketball legends are revered by young and old in Columbus. Names like Jerry Lucas. John Havlicek. Clark Kellogg. Jim Jackson. Each of them a great player who helped to carry on that winning tradition. From the start, my sons respected that heritage and made it clear to anyone who'd listen that they, too, hoped to one day play for the Buckeyes.

Like me, Barbara had majored in education at Oberlin and planned to become a teacher. When we started our family, however, she committed to staying at home, to be with our sons as much as possible. Along with coaching, I continued to teach sociology.

Our decision for Barbara to forego teaching and stay home with the boys for a while involved taking a hard look at our family budget and committing to the sacrifices necessary to survive on my income alone. Among those commitments was continuing to live in the modest home on Columbus's Near East Side where we still reside today. The house is all our sons knew growing up, and remains a source of comfort and great memories to them.

Barbara was raised in a family that stressed effective communication, and she carried that torch. She knows how important it is for any of us, especially young black men, to be able to effectively communicate our thoughts and ideas. She insisted that J.J., at age 6, begin keeping a journal to help him sort out his thoughts and experiences. One of J.J.'s earliest entries in that journal spoke to his desire to play basketball for Ohio State when he was old enough.

Barb and I suspected that, given J.J.'s early exposure to basketball via my coaching, he—and Julian and Jared later--may become passionate about wanting to play. And sure enough, despite Barbara's efforts to introduce him to other interests, from playing saxophone to tap-dancing lessons, it was clear where his desire lay.

Instead of watching cartoons on Saturday mornings like his friends, it wasn't long before J.J. insisted on coming along with me to basketball practices. He picked up the nuances of the game quickly, and it came natural to him. From the earliest, he could shoot well, handle the ball, spot open teammates for a pass and play solid defense. It was obvious to me he had an uncanny early feel for the game. While I was protective of him, I saw how much he loved the game and tried to foster his enthusiasm. He was hungry to compete and prove to himself that he could play.

At seven, J.J. pleaded with us to let him take part in a camp hosted by his favorite former Buckeye player, Jay Burson, a tremendous competitor and scorer for the Buckeyes in the late '80s. Most of the camp's attendees were a few years older than J.J., which further fueled his desire to prove he belonged. With Jay's approval, we agreed to let J.J. participate in the camp on one condition: If the competition proved too much for him to handle, he'd have to stop.

Early in the competition, J.J. took a pass, drove hard to the basket and scored over a taller defender. He got back quickly on defense, stole the ball and zipped a pass to a teammate for an easy layup. He seemed instantly in his comfort zone, and that was that. He thrived at the camp, laying a foundation for what would be a rewarding journey as a player for him.

Turning Around Troubled Programs

My experiences at East High and Franklin University had taught me that, while I loved coaching because of the opportunity to impact young lives, I also thrived on the challenge of taking a downtrodden program and helping to build or rebuild it into something special. As I'd seen at East and Franklin, there were obviously factors beyond a coach's control that could short-circuit even the best-laid plans. But I resolved that it wouldn't deter me from my mission to make a positive difference to youngsters.

I accepted the head coaching job at Beechcroft High School, a beaten-down City League program I hoped to revive. Beechcroft was coming off a horrid 2-19 season. Prior to that, they hadn't won a single game in six years! The program was a laughingstock and had actually become a source of pity among their competitors. As bad as the situation at Beechcroft was when I arrived, I still saw that there was talent in the program. There were plenty of players with skill and potential.

What I *didn't* see, however, was accountability by players to their teammates. The culture of the program had been all about ego, about the *I* instead of the *We*, about players trying to get their own at the expense of their teammates. The idea of accountability, of a family-like team atmosphere where each player was accountable to his teammates, didn't exist.

I began trying to help players understand that just because they all wore the same uniform didn't mean they were a *team*. I tried to help them understand that becoming a true team could happen only when they put aside their egos and began to hold themselves accountable away from the court, embracing their responsibilities at home, at work and in the classroom.

I tried to help them understand that our decisions and actions *off* the court have a direct impact on our ability to perform effectively *on* the court, especially during crunch time, when our true character is revealed. Because *we play the game the way we live our lives*, I told them. The two cannot be separated. If we're taking care of our business off the court, making the right decisions for the right reasons consistently, that sense of confidence, of accountability, will be evident when the heat is on, and we'll thrive. I tried to help them understand that becoming a team meant committing to each other long before they ever put on their uniforms.

Gradually, I began to see improvement in our players' performances. They were taking responsibility away from the court, and it had started to show in practice. They were sharper and more focused. It seemed they had begun to embrace accountability.

We won our first game of the season. Our fans poured out of the stands in celebration, as if we'd won a state championship! It was only one game but, for a program that had enjoyed a grand total of two wins in the previous seven years combined, our victory was a big deal.

Unfortunately, it became too big a deal to our players, who thought the win somehow meant we had arrived as a championship club. They had gotten so used to losing that, when they finally won a game, they suddenly thought they had it all figured out. Instead of using the win as motivation to realize what was possible and keep improving, they became comfortable and temporarily slid back to their old selfish ways. We lost our next few games and the players realized that commitment isn't a sometimes thing. We can succeed only if our effort and attitude is consistently strong and we bring our best each time we take the floor.

That first season at Beechcroft was a huge learning curve, on and off the court, for our players *and* their parents. We were trying to erase a culture of losing and lack of accountability that had been in place for many years, and it wasn't going to happen overnight. Unfortunately for their teammates and coaches, some players simply refuse to go "all in" in their commitment to doing the right things and contributing to something bigger than themselves, no matter how much it may help to improve their game and lives. These players eventually weed themselves out of a program by cutting classes or getting suspended or disrespecting others. They mistakenly assume that being a member of the team is their *right*, rather than a privilege that must be consistently earned.

Sadly, the selfish actions of these players often simply reflect the behavior of their parents, who have failed to set a consistent positive example at home. Players' parents are an important part of any team "family," and can be a huge help or hindrance to a program's progress. Wherever possible, they must do their part to help foster that team-as-family atmosphere. It starts by setting a good example for their kids to follow. It starts with accountability.

On Sundays, our scheduled practice time was at 7 p.m. Not 7:05, or 7:10. 7 p.m. Early on, however, parents of a few players thought it acceptable to drop their kids off at practice late. When those players arrived, they expected to jump right into the flow of practice. I wouldn't allow it. I told them practice had started at 7p.m. and was now closed. They would be unable to practice. Their parents got upset with me, wondered why the players being a "little bit late" to practice was a big deal to me. It was about getting our players, and their parents, to accept accountability. And that accountability works both ways; a coach is accountable to their *players and their players' parents*, too. If practice is supposed to be over at 8 p.m., for example, the coach should have those players walking out the gym door at 8 p.m. Not at 8:05, or 8:10. The parents of those players are expecting to pick up their kids at a certain time, have arranged their schedule to do so, and the coach should respect that and structure practice so that it's over and the kids are ready to leave the gym on time. It's about learning to look beyond our *own* needs and considering what's best for the group, about holding each other accountable while becoming a part of something bigger than ourselves.

Our players began to understand the ingredients necessary to eliminate that loser's mindset that had been prevalent at Beechcroft for so long, and to realize that becoming a good team required each player's best attitude and effort every day, not just sometimes. It required right decision-making and trust in each other, and me, in the name of team. It was up to each of us, players and coaches, to put in the work, and there could be no excuses, no hiding behind those bushes Coach Penn had taught us about back at Oberlin.

We took our lumps early on, but those lumps no longer included lack of pride or effort. Our kids became accustomed to giving it everything they had in every game. Win or lose, they left it all on the court. When we lost a game, it was no longer because we were outworked or outhustled. Players began to embrace their assigned roles, their places in the system. They began to trust each other and me.

Steadily, the program turned around. Within three seasons, a laughingstock program that had been left for dead won our conference division and played in the 1994 Columbus City League Championship game. I was named the Ohio High School Coach of the Year. While I was honored, of course, the award was really about our players and their families, about their commitment and sacrifice and support for each other, for the team's best interests. Our players had finally seen what was possible for them, on the court and off, if they held themselves accountable.

Ego and Excuses

Unfortunately, sometimes in life, even though we know what the right decision is, we make the wrong one, often due to selfishness. And it costs us. It goes back to accountability, to making the right decisions for the right reasons consistently. Sometimes we learn lessons the hard way. Hopefully, we become better for it. That's what happened to the best player on our team at Beechcroft High that season.

The day before a big game, a game with the conference division title at stake, our star player missed practice. He said it was because he'd had an argument with his girlfriend. I suspended him for the game. His father was upset and challenged me. "If you suspend him for this game," his father said, "Beechcroft may lose the game and the division title. Why don't you let him play in this game and suspend him for the next one, instead?" I stood firm. "But your son missed practice for *this* game," I told him. "So, unfortunately, *this* is the game he'll have to sit out."

As a team, we always talked about the importance of accountability, of making the right choices on and off the court. It was the only way we could build trust in each other, trust that would translate during crunch time of the biggest games. *You play the game the way you live your lives*, I told them. We couldn't expect to make the wrong decisions off the court and yet thrive on the court. Karma wouldn't let us. Now, our best player had missed practice the day before a big game and had let his teammates down. As a coach, I could either stand strong for the core values our club represented or break weak and let him play, just to win a damned ballgame. There could be no compromise.

Our star player sat on the bench the whole game. But our team overcame the adversity and played with passion and purpose. We won the game and clinched the division championship with our best player sitting on the bench. I was proud of the way our players stepped up for each other despite difficult circumstances.

A few years later, after our star player went on to enjoy success as a college player, he and I were chatting one day and he thanked me for suspending him for that game. He said his suspension had proved a turning point for him where his attitude and ego were concerned. He told me that, in hindsight, he was convinced that if I had allowed him to play in that big game after he'd missed practice for it, he'd have been on a bad path to becoming a "basketball tramp," a player without values.

Fierce Brotherly Pride

As my coaching career progressed, our family expanded. Our second son, Julian, was born. Though four years younger than J.J., Julian wasn't about to take a backseat to his older brother. Like J.J., Julian showed strong early interest in basketball and intense desire to compete. He tagged along with J.J. to rough-and-tumble neighborhood pickup games. J.J. didn't cut him slack, either, never let the other kids take it easy on his younger brother, and that's the way Julian wanted it. From the outset, Julian had to earn his way with J.J. If he couldn't take the pounding, J.J. told him, stay home. And there was plenty of pounding.

Those neighborhood battles on the court were fierce, and the boys often returned home bruised and bloody. But they loved it. They understood the physical toll was just part of the game and whining or complaining was a waste of time. The intensity from those neighborhood games often spilled over to scraps between the boys at home, too, and neither gave an inch. They wanted badly to beat each other, and the loser heard about it. Even in Nerf basketball.

They'd hang one basket from the top of their bedroom door and the other from mine and Barb's, and they'd battle for hours in the narrow hallway. Despite their scuffles, one thing was unmistakable: There was a bond between them that nothing could penetrate. They were proud of each other and tried to bring out the best in one another. It's still that way. Julian developed a tenacity and resiliency in trying to keep up with J.J. that would prove helpful to him while facing adversity as a high school and college player later on.

The Importance of Listening

Barb held down the fort at home. She is a strong woman and great mom, and she was always there for our boys, pushing them in their studies, supporting them during their struggles, feeding them confidence and encouragement. She fostered the closeness we enjoy with our sons today. Barb is tough, but she's always had a soft touch, too, and an ability to connect with our sons on a more delicate, emotional level.

I was always harder-edged, a "tough love" father, quick to put the hammer down on our sons if I suspected they were off track even slightly. While discipline is a key to the game in raising children, the way it's delivered can be tricky. From a physical perspective, it's safe to say there's nothing delicate about me. I'm 6'7", often animated, with a booming voice like my dad's and, whether with my players or students or sons, it's generally hard to miss my presence.

While my sons were growing up, the combination of my size and abrupt approach became a source of fear to them. Sometimes I found myself parenting through intimidation, and that's a bad place to be. As a parent, the last thing we want is for our kids to be afraid of us. Because then, they'll start keeping their troubles bottled up instead of sharing them with us so we can solve those problems together. It cuts off a crucial outlet for them and they begin to withdraw. It's critical to keep that line of communication open with them.

There's nothing better than knowing our kids feel comfortable coming to us for advice about things that are happening in their lives, knowing they trust our judgment. Or that, at the very least, they're willing to listen to our ideas. It was always that way for our sons with Barb, but not so much with me. It took time for me to understand and adjust, to tone down my authoritative approach with our sons and begin to truly *listen* to what they were saying without declaring that I already had all the answers. When kids trust us enough to open up to us, it's our duty to listen and try to understand. If we're truly listening to them, we can hear the amazing development going on in their minds. Most of the time, they already know what the answers are. They just need to know that we're listening. It took time for my sons to let their guard down and feel they could talk with me about things they were dealing with.

We should always strive to be better parents and not ever think we have all the answers. No matter how much we may think we know, we can always learn more, and we're obligated to our kids to keep trying to get better.

Burying Bitterness and a Wrong Coaching Move

My father's sudden reappearance in my life after I'd graduated from college was emotionally tough for me to handle at first. Despite the bitterness I still felt about the way he treated my mom and me all those years, I decided to push that resentment aside and forge a new relationship with him. Slowly, I allowed him to be part of my life.

I refused, however, to hear his excuses for his actions in the past. He'd done what he'd done, I figured, so there was no use discussing it. It wouldn't change anything. While I knew our relationship could never be what I longed for as a kid, I believed it was important for my sons to get to know their grandfather, to understand that key family piece that had been missing for so long and have an opportunity to build their own relationships with him. And, to his credit, he became a wonderful grandfather to them.

After helping to take a Beechcroft High team that had won *a total* of two games in seven seasons before I arrived to a division champion that was battling for the City League title a few years later, I began to hear from other schools about their coaching situations, including down-and-out programs like Beechcroft's had been. While I hadn't anticipated leaving Beechcroft after helping to turn things around and build a winning foundation there, I found myself attracted to the challenge of trying to do it again elsewhere, to trying to help rebuild another struggling program. So I accepted the head coaching job at Reynoldsburg High School. It was a move I would regret.

I became the first black head coach at Reynoldsburg High, which mattered not to me when I took the job. Soon enough, however, having a black coach and, eventually, black players seemed to matter much to some in the community, who were resistant to it and began making things difficult for the rest of us. Parents of a few white players who felt their sons weren't getting a fair shake from me, who believed I favored black players, complained publicly to school administrators, seeking my removal as coach. The truth was, I favored any damned player, white or black or green, who showed the desire and ability and commitment necessary to help the team, period. Those winning traits in a player are color-blind. Unfortunately, I've found over the years that parents of players, in looking at their son's or daughter's team purely from a subjective viewpoint, expect coaches to start their child and the "other best four" players, regardless of what's truly best for the team.

It was a troubling situation for me at Reynoldsburg from the outset, and, despite my hope that it would turn around, the atmosphere in the community toward the reality of a black coach and black players only worsened. The tumult took a toll on our program. A simple show of support for me by the school principal likely would have eased the unrest, but it wasn't to be. Instead, the principal pushed aside the idea of doing the right thing so he could avoid further ruffling the feathers of a frustrated few, and the proverbial writing on the wall was clear for me to read.

A Father's Unintentional Lessons

While I was in the midst of turbulent circumstances at Reynoldsburg, my dad suffered a heart attack and died. As I said, despite our issues, he had become a terrific grandfather to my sons. J.J. was a teenager when he died, Julian was 9, and our youngest, Jared, was 3. In some ways, it seemed my father had been trying to make up for time lost with me through his relationship with my boys, and I encouraged it. Watching him spend time with them made me feel like a kid again, too, and made me feel that, finally, I was included in his love. For the first time in our relationship, he was *there*. When he died, I knew the yearning I always had for him to walk through the door and say the things I wanted to hear as a son would never be fulfilled, and the finality of it was brutal for me.

It may seem strange, but I'm actually thankful to my dad for the lessons he taught me. I learned much about being a father through his absence. I learned a lot from his mistakes, learned how *not* to treat my kids if I hoped to be a great father someday.

His absence in my life all those years, and the emptiness I felt because of it, fueled my desire to be there for my sons with the love and support all kids deserve. My dad helped me realize what being a real father means. While I'll never understand the decisions he made as a father, I don't fault him for them anymore. I had to let it go. At some point, we all have to let it go, have to rid ourselves of that emotional baggage we're dragging. Before he died, I was able to open up to him, to apologize for the bitterness I'd carried toward him for so long, to thank him for what he had taught me. I tried to explain it all, but I don't think he understood what I meant about the lessons I'd learned from him.

I believe there are lessons from God tucked in all of our experiences and we can seek to find and learn from them or ignore them. I'm thankful for the lessons my dad taught me, and have tried to use them for good in my relationship with my sons. I know too well what it could've been like for my sons if I'd gone in the same direction my dad did. My sons and I don't always see eye-to-eye, but one thing's for sure: I'll always let them know how much I love them, and I'll always be there for them.

You Can't Go Home Again

As the situation deteriorated at Reynoldsburg, I received a phone call from the athletic director at Oberlin College, my alma mater. Oberlin needed a new basketball coach and the athletic director was interested in hiring me for the job. Oberlin has always been a special place to me and is where I learned important lessons about life from Coach Pat Penn. Oberlin was the beginning of a second chance for me as a student and basketball player in the mid '70s, after I'd succumbed to street life and gotten in trouble and narrowly avoided prison. Coach Penn had come to my aid back then, had helped me through legal problems and brought me to Oberlin, letting me know it was time to sink or swim; he told me that if I planned to live a life of purpose, there could be no more excuses.

Oberlin is where I met Barbara. It's where I enjoyed success as a player, including being named captain and becoming part of the most successful team in school history at the time. As a student, Oberlin helped me to expand my thinking, to look beyond the obvious in situations and consider other angles or perspectives. I'm grateful for all of it. My experiences at Oberlin changed my life. But you know that old saying, "You can't go home again"? From a professional standpoint, I was about to learn what it meant.

I returned to Oberlin College as head basketball coach in 1997, carrying the torch for everything Pat Penn had taught me as a player there, for character and commitment and accountability to self and team. Oberlin's program had been in the basement for several years, winning only two games the previous season, and I knew I had my work cut out for me if I hoped to turn the program around. I quickly realized, however, the Oberlin College I had known as a student and player was nowhere to be found. The culture of the university had changed dramatically over the years, altered by leaders who'd come from elsewhere and had little regard for Oberlin's proud heritage. I found a basketball program there that was barely breathing, hamstrung by players and a school administration living in fantasyland where real competition at the college level was concerned. The refusal by administrators at Oberlin to even consider, much less approve, changes necessary to revamp a dying program dumbfounded me.

For starters, the administration decided that new male students interested in playing basketball at Oberlin who claimed even the slightest previous experience should be considered "recruits" by me for the team. At best, these so-called recruits had played a little club-level basketball and were a world away talent-wise from even an average small-college player. The accompanying lack of effort and understanding from these players of what was necessary to compete at the college level was incredibly frustrating for me.

My frustration boiled over one day during practice, when a lollygagging player asked why we even had to practice at *all*, wondered aloud why we couldn't just focus on the games and have fun instead. My response to him was direct: We'd practice as hard as possible to get better and put ourselves in the best position to win. If he couldn't make the necessary commitment, I told him, he was free to leave and not return. Rather than simply quitting, however, the player complained to the president of Oberlin about my "overbearing" practice methods. The president backed the player and told me that unless all players on the team agreed with the way we practiced, I would not be permitted to hold practice.

Suffice to say, the basketball program at Oberlin didn't stand a chance. I lasted three seasons as coach there, fulfilling my contract, and resigned. We went 3-21 in my first season, 2-22 in my last. The losing was brutal but to me, the administration's indifference toward the program was worse.

I didn't fault the kids. Most of our players were foisted on the program by school administration and were in over their heads from the start. They were "club players," intramural players who were overmatched across the board. They had no clue what was necessary to compete at the college level, nor inclination to learn and do it. Losing had become part of the program's fabric at Oberlin and had become acceptable. It was OK to lose all the time, it seemed, as long as the players were having fun. Unlike the special years I enjoyed as a student and player there, Oberlin was no longer the place for me.

THIRD QUARTER

J.J. Realizes a Buckeye Dream

In 2001, following a strong high school career, J.J. received a scholarship offer from the legendary Nolan Richardson to play basketball at Arkansas. Coach Richardson had led the Razorbacks to three Final Fours and the 1994 national championship. J.J. was excited to play in Coach Richardson's intense and up-tempo system, known as "40 minutes of Hell," a reference to the challenge opposing teams faced against the Razorbacks' relentless pressure.

J.J. enjoyed a solid freshman season at Arkansas and developed a great relationship with Coach Richardson. When Coach Richardson was fired after the season, however, J.J. decided to look elsewhere for opportunity. Jim O'Brien, then coach at Ohio State, offered him a scholarship and a chance to return home and realize his dream of playing for the Buckeyes. That journal entry J.J. had written as a

J.J., my eldest son, realized his dream of playing for the hometown Buckeyes.
(photo courtesy of Dispatch Printing Company)

young boy about someday playing for the Buckeyes was about to become reality.

Due to his transfer, J.J. was forced to sit out the '02-'03 season, but played for the Buckeyes for three seasons. Playing at Ohio State was a terrific experience for J.J. all the way around. He was back at home, where family and friends could watch his games in person. He was part of a team that won the Big Ten Conference championship in 2005-06. He played two seasons for Coach Thad Matta, who replaced Jim O'Brien. Coach Matta is regarded by many as one of the best coaches in the country. J.J. averaged double figures in scoring for a season twice, and narrowly missed it a third.

More importantly, J.J. earned a degree from Ohio State and developed relationships while there that will last a lifetime. His days at Ohio State afforded J.J. the opportunity to play professional basketball overseas, to experience a variety of cultures and visit parts of the world he likely otherwise would never have seen. J.J. played for teams in China, Poland, Austria and Belgium. It was a wonderful life growth experience for him. Another byproduct of J.J. playing at Ohio State was the positive impact it had on Jared, who, at 12 or 13, had begun to accompany J.J. to practices and open gyms. During open gyms in the summer, Jared was tossed into the competitive fire, playing against guys many years older than he, guys like J.J. who played college ball at Ohio State or elsewhere. Some of the players were professionals. Those experiences fueled Jared's desire to compete at a high level.

Don't Let Your Past Define Your Future

Though I had avoided prison for my missteps with drugs as a young man, my troubles continued to hold me emotional hostage. I was a teacher and coach, working with kids and fulfilling what

I believed was God's purpose for my life, but was still haunted by my poor decisions from the past.

I tried to block out that troubled period of my life, tried to pretend I hadn't made those bad decisions that negatively impacted my teammates and me. I tried to make believe the "old me" had never existed. It didn't work. My anxiety overwhelmed me and I sought professional help.

I underwent therapy to deal with my inner turmoil, and it was an awakening for me. I learned to look at my past in a new way, realized I couldn't hide from my mistakes or pretend I hadn't made them. I learned that mistakes from the past didn't have to define my future in a negative way.

When our sons were young, I shared with them my bad decision to take a shortcut and get involved with drugs. I explained to them how my choice had almost cost me everything, and that I'd paid a steep emotional price for it. By God's grace, I said, I'd been given a second chance to live with purpose and lead with passion, and I had tried ever since to make the most of it.

Telling my sons about my struggles was painful and embarrassing for me, but I refused to hide it from them. I wanted them to know I'd made mistakes and that I'd learned and grown from those mistakes. I believed my sons could learn from my experiences, that my story might help them avoid similar temptations or pitfalls. I wanted my sons to know that so-called "shortcuts" are really just dead-end roads. And they can take you to trouble fast.

Home at Last

My dream of leading my alma mater, Oberlin, back to basketball respectability had died in the face of the administration's apathetic approach to the program, so I returned to Columbus in 2000 as head coach at Northland High School. By that time, I had developed a track record as a nomad coach, staying at a school for a few years and moving on. Barbara joked that I was becoming a sort of "Larry Brown of high school basketball," a reference to the well-traveled former NBA and college coach with a penchant for turning around programs in decline, then moving to another job. I welcomed the notion of a parallel with Coach Brown because he is a winner. But I knew what she really meant.

In reality, there were many reasons I'd left the places I had coached after brief stays. I was at peace with all of them. We had turned around a progam of questionable character at East High, were headed toward consistent success there until a scheming principal decided winning meant more than integrity and paid with his job because of it. At Franklin University, the death of the university president shortly after I arrived changed the game in a heartbeat, from his belief in and support for a fledgling program to the disdain and denial of resources by his successor. At Beechcroft High, our turnaround from laughingstock to contender was swift, and the program was on a championship track when I departed. My experience as coach at Reynoldsburg was a stark reminder of the ugliness of racial divide, and was, in retrospect, a poor choice by me to take the job. And at Oberlin, despite my best efforts to revamp a sunken program, it was clear to me the administration's laughable approach to college-level sports would prohibit any possible progress.

As I said, I believe that for any relationship to work, including a job, three things have to be in place. First, we must *understand our partners*, the environment we're in and the conditions that affect the relationship. Second, we must feel that *we're understood*, that our teammates or coaches or bosses understand our approach and commitment to the task. And third, we must feel that we're *wanted*, that our teammates or coaches or bosses value our commitment and efforts to help the team succeed. A relationship will ultimately prove unsuccessful if there is failure in any of these three areas.

I took the reins of a Northland High program that was beaten, bruised and had been a Columbus City League doormat for several years. My mission out of the gate at Northland was to establish a foundation of trust by the players in themselves and each other, and in me as their coach. Most of the players at Northland had never been asked to hold themselves accountable for anything, had no idea what it meant. They had done what they wanted, when they wanted, on and off the court, without having to answer for their actions.

It was my job to help them understand that those bad decisions away from the court had everything to do with lack of success on it, that karma wouldn't let them win if they weren't handling their business. If they were taking shortcuts in class, at work, at home, not treating themselves or others with respect, they couldn't expect to perform well during crunch time on the court. Again, I told them, *you play the game the way you live your life.* The way they played when the game was on the line would reflect the way they were handling themselves off the court. The two were inseparable. If they were making the right decisions off the court, their practicing of accountability would shine through during crunch time. When pressure knocks on our door, the way we've been living our lives is exposed and there's nowhere for us to hide.

The first few seasons at Northland were tough, and we measured progress in small steps. Before we could begin to win, we first had to learn *how* to do it. For me, a key part of learning how was helping kids understand the importance of commitment to improvement in the off-season. As a team, we could work as hard as possible *during* the season, but it was up to each player individually to do the work to keep improving *after* the season. I've always believed that *teams* are made during the season (November through March), but *players* are made in the off-season, from March until November.

Early in my tenure at Northland, I received word that Pat Penn, my coach at Oberlin College and a man who had believed in me and taught me how to live with purpose and helped me to turn my life around, had died. I reflected on everything I had learned from Coach Penn, all those lessons that went way beyond basketball, lessons about accountability and selflessness that still guide me today. I felt tremendous gratitude for all he'd done for me. I figured that, as a coach, if I were lucky enough to impact even one player the way Coach Penn had impacted me, my career would be a success.

It was a work in progress, but our Northland program steadily began to turn around. Guys started to understand and accept their roles, began to hold themselves and each other accountable. Steadily, our club progressed from losing all games we played against favored teams and some games we played against lesser teams, to winning some games against favored teams and most of our games against lesser teams, to winning most games against favored teams and all games against underdogs. Finally, we reached a level where we were considered a heavy favorite in just about any game we played.

Foundation for Excellence

A highlight of those early years at Northland for me was being fortunate to coach my son Julian. Julian and his teammates experienced lots of losing in the beginning, but he was among a group of players who laid the vital first bricks in what became a winning foundation. Losing was unacceptable to Julian and his teammates, and they helped to establish a tone of discipline and accountability for those who followed, including Jared. During Julian's senior season in 2003-04, our club finished 14-7, unspectacular but a far cry from the losing records that had been prevalent at Northland for so long. The program turned a corner that season and would soon be headed for a remarkable run to the national spotlight.

Julian was an All-City League performer as a senior, and hoped to play Division I college ball. He was tenacious and versatile as a player, willing to fill any role to help his team win games. He could do a little of everything, from hitting a jumper to grabbing a key rebound to playing in-your-face defense, but he prided himself on his toughness. He was a smart player, too, with strong court awareness. At 6'4", though, Julian's height was a concern to many D-1 programs that thought him undersized.

Julian enrolled at Fork Union Military Academy, a prep school in Virginia, for a year, hoping to add an inch or two to his frame while there. He led the team in scoring and rebounding, but

scholarship offers from D-1 programs remained scarce. He grew frustrated, but refused to let it get the best of him. Julian knew that no matter what happened, the two things he could always control were his effort and his attitude. He accepted a scholarship offer to play for Kent State University and Coach Jim Christian, who won at least twenty games every season he coached the Golden Flashes.

Julian played forward at Kent State and was a part of three MAC championship teams. He also enjoyed the

Julian was fortunate to be a part of three MAC Championship teams while playing at Kent State.
(photo courtesy of Kent State University Athletic Dept.)

thrill of playing in the NCAA tournament. Though his playing time varied, the determination and resiliency he learned while trying to keep up with older brother J.J. in those pickup games as a boy always showed. Whenever Julian was called upon at Kent State, he answered with outstanding effort, setting a great example for his teammates.

Julian also set a good example for Jared, who was inspired to see his older brothers overcome adversity, first J.J. in dealing with Coach Richardson's firing at Arkansas and subsequent transfer to Ohio State, where he was forced to sit out a year, then Julian in fighting to prove he belonged at the Division 1 level. From the earliest, Jared longed to follow in their footsteps as a strong player with a team-first, whatever-it-takes attitude.

As I said, our program at Northland High had turned a corner, and we were full steam ahead down what would be a dominant track. Jared would play a key role in that run.

Hungry to Prove Himself

With a coach for a father and older brothers who played the game at a high level, Jared had perhaps been groomed for basketball success. Respect for the game has always been part of our family heritage, from my father's days as a player with the Sioux City Colored Ghosts to my brother Brief's days as a high-school All-American in New Jersey, from my passion for coaching to J.J.'s and Julian's experiences at Ohio State and Kent State, respectively. Jared intended to carry that Sullinger family competitive torch.

Long before he tagged along with J.J. to practices at Ohio State and played against professionals at open gyms as a teen, Jared showed the potential to become a special player. When he was two, I started tossing little post passes to him at the foot of his bed, giving him his first taste of proper footwork. When he was three, he was able to shoot a regulation free throw with a men's ball. He was already strong enough to hold the ball and follow through on the shot. At five, he could shoot from the three-point line and make a few. At six, Jared attempted a crossover dribble in a youth league game. He was trying to be flashy. While I let him know later there was no place in the game for showboating, it was an example of his early confidence in his abilities.

Jared was pudgy as a kid and battled weight problems that were tough on him emotionally at times, but his belief in himself on the court never wavered. He had strong hands and displayed excellent footwork. He knew how to position himself effectively around the basket and make the most of his opportunities. Even as a kid, he had a great feel for the game.

He insisted on competing with his brothers in neighborhood pickup games and at home, and J.J. and Julian were relentless with him. They exposed Jared to the physical part of basketball and he quickly learned that whining or crying about contact was useless. If you got knocked down, he learned, you got up and kept playing. To be accepted by his brothers, Jared knew he'd have to earn it, like Julian had earned J.J.'s competitive respect before him.

One day, Jared went with J.J. to Little Marvin's Court, a neighborhood court where the battles were fierce. Bragging rights were always at stake, so you'd better bring your best game. J.J. and Jared teamed up in a game of two-on-two. With the score tied, J.J. drove to the basket and Jared's defender slid over to guard J.J., leaving Jared uncovered. J.J. dished the ball to Jared for what should have been an easy game-winning layup. Jared fumbled the pass, however, and he and J.J. eventually lost the game.

J.J. was furious with Jared for dropping that pass, and he let Jared hear about it all the way home. The two of them spent the next few hours in the front yard, with J.J. firing up-close passes at Jared. Some of the passes bounced off Jared's hands and hit him in the face, but he took what his older brother dished out, knowing that J.J. was just trying to help him improve. To this day, J.J. still jokes that he deserves credit for helping Jared develop quick reflexes and strong hands on the court.

That experience was among many "tough love" moments for Jared in competing with his brothers, and all of them helped to develop his grit and sense of purpose on the court. Jared believes in himself and doesn't hide when crunch time comes.

Jared's body grew quickly and he continued to improve. When he was in eighth grade, he received a scholarship offer from Tommy Amaker, then coach at Michigan. Suffice to say, after being born and raised on the Buckeyes, Jared playing for Michigan wouldn't happen. Following Georgetown's upset of Ohio State in the 2006 NCAA tournament, an emotional J.J. told Jared that if Ohio State coach Thad Matta ever offered him a scholarship, Jared should accept it and not think twice. J.J. believed strongly in Coach Matta and the direction of his program.

As a freshman at Northland High in 2007, Jared received that scholarship offer from Coach Matta, and accepted it. It appeared Jared's dream of becoming a Buckeye would come true.

Big Game, Bigger Lesson

First, however, he had a lot to learn at Northland, much of which had little to do with basketball. Jared was our tallest player at 6'7" and was ready to test himself in varsity competition. He had always thrived on playing against older guys, starting with J.J. and Julian. Jared wore No. 34 at Northland to honor Julian, who wore No. 34 at Northland and Kent State. Julian had been among the first wave of players at Northland to help raise the program from the depths and set it on a winning track.

We rolled through the regular season undefeated that year and captured the first of what would be five consecutive City League championships. Our team was a great mix of veteran leadership and young talent. Among our leaders was guard Devon Moore, a second-team All-Ohio selection who went on to become a tremendous player, and leader, at James Madison University. Several of our key players that season were freshmen or sophomores. There's only one way to become experienced at anything, and that's by being inexperienced the first time you do it. Then, you just keep doing it.

Jared learned some valuable life lessons at Northland High.
(photo courtesy of Dispatch Printing Company)

We lost in the regional semifinals, and finished 24-1. Our young guys played lots of minutes that season, including those tense moments late in games, and learned what crunch time was all about. They were talented and hungry to improve. Though Jared didn't start for us as a freshman, he was still good enough to be named first-team All-City and All-District, and was a second-team All-Ohio selection. He knew he had to keep improving, however, especially where his physical strength was concerned. He started to understand the importance of conditioning, and he began hitting the weight room regularly.

During his sophomore season at Northland in 2008-09, Jared learned a crucial life lesson that cost him, and our team, plenty. It was a lesson about the real meaning of accountability, and the lesson he learned still motivates Jared. We rolled through the regular season undefeated again, were 21-0 entering a district semifinal game. Jared had played a major role in our success to that point, becoming one of the dominant high school post players in the country. He had become our go-to guy. As the season progressed, however, Jared began to slack off in his schoolwork. I learned he had been late turning in a class assignment, and I shared my disappointment with him, from a father's and coach's perspective. I reminded him of his obligation to his teachers, his teammates and himself. I let him know that if it happened again, he'd be suspended immediately for a game, no matter when or how big that game may be.

On the day of our district semifinal game, I found out Jared had again been late turning in his homework. He'd left me no choice.

I informed him that he was suspended from our tournament game that night and that he wouldn't be allowed to wear his uniform while sitting on the bench. He was crushed. After the first classroom episode, he had promised it wouldn't happen again. But it did. He claimed he understood accountability, but his actions showed otherwise. He had ignored the critical connection between his actions off the court and their impact on him and his teammates on the court. Jared realized he had let his teammates down when they needed him most. He had let his community down, himself and his family down. He had failed to hold himself accountable.

I suspended Jared for that tournament game based on what I believed were his best interests as a young man, not as a basketball player. I'd have made the same decision with any of my players in that situation, no matter how talented they might be. What was best for him at that moment had nothing to do with basketball. It was far beyond wins and losses. It was about a crucial life lesson, about values that would shape his future as a father or husband or neighbor or employee.

We lost the game, and our hopes for a possible state championship were gone. Afterward, tears flowed in the locker room. It was the last game for our seniors and it was a bitter and unexpected way for them to go out. Jared was devastated that he'd let those seniors down. He knew he could never make it up to them. He had let his selfishness interfere with the good of the team.

I've never second-guessed my decision to suspend Jared for that game, even though it impacted teammates who had done nothing wrong. That part of it bothered me terribly. But I believe that to succeed in life, accountability can't be an occasional thing. Though it was tough for our other players, especially those seniors, they respected my decision. They understood I'd have made the same decision if it had been any of them, too; I refused to look the other way just because it was my son or our best player. I wanted to win, of course, but *not* if it meant sweeping an important character lesson for a young man under the table. Our players realized that, as members of a team, they were all a part of something bigger than any of them individually. That's what "team" is all about.

After that incident, Jared became accountable. He was never late turning in class assignments again and he thrived as a student at Northland High and later at Ohio State. Jared learned that accountability means handling our responsibilities consistently, doing the right things for the right reasons each time, not just when it's convenient for us. He had learned the difference between commitment and convenience. He had realized that no matter how many points he scored or rebounds he grabbed in a game, being a good teammate went way beyond the basketball court.

CRUNCH TIME

Coming Through in Crunch Time

When Jared was a junior, all the pieces were in place at Northland for us to make a state championship run. Our team had great size, quickness, depth and court savvy. Trey Burke, the 2012-13 consensus national college player of the year who led Michigan to the NCAA Championship game, was our point guard. As a freshman at Northland, Trey had learned the ropes at point guard from Devon Moore, who taught him what toughness and determination was all about, and he was ready to assume the mantel for us. Dimonde Hale, who went on to become one of the all-time leading scorers at Denison University, was at one wing. J.D. Weatherspoon, who played a season at Ohio State with Jared before transferring to Toledo, was at the other. Javon Cornley, who went on to become a starting defensive end at Indiana, controlled the paint with Jared.

We lost one game during the regular season, in overtime, and entered the state tournament hungry and focused. We won our first few tournament games in decisive fashion, but then the games got tighter, each one going to the wire. Our guys prided themselves on coming through during crunch time, on staying in the moment, on controlling the two things any of us always have control over: our effort and attitude.

The players knew if they were thinking about that turnover they'd made or a foul they'd committed on the previous possession, they would squander the present moment, which was the only one they could affect. The way our players thrived during crunch time was a reflection of how they were taking care of their business off the court. They understood it goes hand in hand, and that karma shone through when it mattered most. Because *you play the game the way you live your life*.

We won the state championship game in dramatic fashion. Jared sank a couple of free throws with two seconds left, breaking a tie, and our opponent, Cincinnati Princeton, missed a floor-length shot as the buzzer sounded. It was the first state championship in Northland basketball history. Afterward, as I reflected on our special season, I thought about how far our program had come over the years, how much our players had sacrificed to help build the program from those lean early years. We built the program "brick by brick," and each of our players represented an important piece of what had become a strong foundation for sustainable success. To me, our state championship represented what winning the right way meant. Each player knew they were a part of something bigger than themselves and owed a debt of gratitude to their teammates and those who had come before them.

Winning the banner games can only happen with commitment and true teamwork.
(photo courtesy of Dispatch Printing Company)

You Can Never Take It For Granted

In 2009-10, we entered the season ranked by *USA Today* as one of the top teams in the country. In a span of a few weeks early in the season, we beat perennial national powerhouses Findlay Prep (Henderson, Nevada), 53-52, and Oak Hill Academy (Mouth of Wilson, Virginia), 47-46. Findlay Prep and Oak Hill had finished the previous season ranked first and second, respectively, in the *USA Today* poll. Both games were televised on *ESPN*, which added to the electric atmosphere.

In 2009-10, our Northland High program rose to national prominence.

Findlay Prep featured current NBA players Tristan Thompson and Cory Joseph, and entered their game against us riding a 45-game winning streak. They were averaging more than 100 points a game. Our players knew it would take an incredible defensive effort to slow Findlay Prep, and they delivered. In the face of our relentless defensive pressure, Findlay Prep scored just 15 points in the first half. Trey Burke did a tremendous job defensively, holding Joseph, who'd been averaging 26 points a game, to just 8. Trey is a special player, as he proved en route to becoming the Big Ten Player of the Year as a sophomore at Michigan and an NBA Lottery Pick. Trey can do it all on the court. He can go left or right, catch and shoot, shoot off the bounce, penetrate and kick, penetrate and finish, pass well and play great defense. But most importantly, he has great character and an excellent work ethic. He's a winner. He prepares to win and he's not afraid to take that big shot in crunch time. Jared prides himself on thriving in big games, too, and scored 32 points and pulled down 21 rebounds against Findlay Prep.

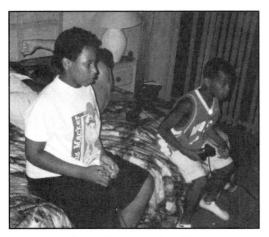

True to their brotherhood, Jared and Trey have always competed off the court, too.

Jared and Trey have a special relationship. In essence, they're like brothers. They hit it off instantly when they began playing ball together as youngsters and have been close friends ever since. They became teammates for the first time when Jared was seven and Trey six, playing on an AAU team coached by Trey's father, Benji. They were teammates on Benji's squad for several years. They also played together at Monroe Middle School in Columbus for one season, and the team went undefeated. When Trey was in eighth grade, his family moved to Atlanta. They returned to Columbus a year later, and Trey and Jared reunited as teammates at Northland High. As youngsters, they loved to compete against each other at everything. They also got into their share of hijinks together. I arrived home one time and discovered my bedroom window had been broken. I asked Jared and Trey about it, since they'd been hanging out at the house. At first, Jared claimed he'd accidentally kicked the window.

Then, they told me the truth: Trey had thrown a ball at Jared, Jared had ducked and the ball smashed the window. Another time, they were fooling around and

As teammates from youth basketball through their time at Northland High School, Jared and Trey enjoyed much success together.

Trey swung and hit Jared square in the nose. Jared's nose started to bleed and Trey came scrambling up the stairs, all too aware of the enormous size difference between them, especially as kids.

Against Oak Hill, led by Doron Lamb, now playing in the NBA, J.D. Weatherspoon handled the dirty work inside for us, scoring 21 points in an ugly, hard-fought win. In both games, our players were able to block out the hype and focus on their responsibilities in the moment.

With those wins, Northland High became the first public school ever to be ranked No. 1 in the *USA Today* Super 25 poll, and we were considered heavy favorites to capture a second consecutive state championship. We finished the regular season unbeaten and were ranked as the top team in the nation entering the state tournament. We rolled through the district round, but lost to an undefeated Gahanna team in a regional semifinal. Gahanna simply overwhelmed us. They were the aggressors, had us back on our heels from the start, and we failed to respond. They seized control of the game in the second quarter and kept the hammer down. They shot 60 percent from the field for the game. We never threatened.

Just like that, our season was over, our hopes of winning a second straight state championship and mythical national championship dashed. We had let our guard down against a good team and hadn't played with that urgency and focus we prided ourselves on and it cost us. Our players were crushed, believing they had failed themselves and the

Jared's last home game at Northland High.

Northland community. I understood their disappointment. I was disappointed, too. But I told our players that we could hold our heads high, that there was no shame in losing to a good team. After all, Gahanna had entered that contest undefeated, too. The game was a painful reminder for us that in life and sports, there is often little margin for error. No matter how talented we may be, if we don't bring our best each time out, we're risking defeat.

Individual Awards Equal 'Team'

It was another dominant season for Jared, as he averaged 23 points and 12 rebounds a game. Our team had been fortunate to pull ahead by large margins early in many games, so Jared and our other starters sat out the second halves of those games. As a coach, those were golden opportunities to get our younger players valuable experience. Like any competitor, Jared hated being pulled from games. He led the cheers for his teammates, but he preferred being on the court every possible minute.

Jared was named the Naismith National High School Player of the Year in the spring of 2010, and that same year I was named Naismith National High School Coach of the Year. It's the only time a father and son have been named Naismith Coach and Player of the year, respectively. While it was a great honor for Jared and me, the recognition we received was a direct result of the success of our whole team, a tribute to the efforts of the entire group. That's what made it special. Jared knew that without his teammates passing the ball to him or setting a pick for him or contributing to all those wins, it wouldn't have happened. I knew my Coach of the Year Award was simply a reflection of how hard our players had worked, of how they had trusted me and bought into the program and become accountable to themselves and each other. Our awards were truly about the power of teamwork. Individual awards always are. No one gets there without help from others.

In 2010, Jared and I were humbled to be named the Naismith National High School Player and Coach of the Year, respectively. The awards were a direct result of the commitment to purpose all of our players displayed.
(photo courtesy of Atlanta Tipoff Club)

Freshman Expectations

As a freshman at Ohio State, Jared's dream of becoming a Buckeye had become reality. He chose to wear No. 0 as a tribute to J.J., who also wore No. 0 for the Buckeyes. Jared was part of a highly-touted recruiting class for the Buckeyes that included point guard Aaron Craft and wing players Lenzelle Smith Jr. and Deshaun Thomas. Jared's former teammate at Northland, J.D. Weatherspoon, was also part of that group.

The Buckeyes were a talented, experienced team, led by seniors David Lighty and Jon Diebler. They had been through the Big Ten battles and knew what it took to win a conference championship. Led by national player of the year Evan Turner, the Buckeyes had won the Big Ten Tournament, finished as conference co-champions and made it to the Sweet Sixteen in the NCAA tournament the previous season.

Jared started at forward as a freshman for the Buckeyes, who began the season ranked in the top-five in the country. He was surrounded in the starting lineup by Lighty, Diebler, senior Dallas Lauderdale and junior William Buford. As he had during all those years of getting knocked on his rear playing against his older brothers, Jared felt right at home playing with and against older players. As always, he expected much from himself. He was being counted upon by his veteran teammates and Coach Matta to produce, and he refused to let them down. Jared knew the accolades he'd received as a player back at Northland High meant nothing now, and he intended to learn and reprove himself at the major college level.

In an early-season battle of top-ten teams, the Buckeyes faced the Gators at Florida. Ohio State won the game handily, thanks to a total team effort. While Lighty, Buford and Diebler did the damage outside, Jared was too much for Florida's big men inside, scoring 26 points and grabbing 10 rebounds. Buford and Craft did a great job of breaking Florida's press, which led to several easy baskets underneath for Jared.

Within a couple of weeks, the Buckeyes were ranked second in the country. They traveled to Florida State, always a tough place to play. Unlike the game against Florida, which had been a fast-paced, up-and-down the court affair, the Florida State game was all about defense. Neither team shot well from outside, and the Buckeyes won the game by controlling the paint. Jared did his part inside with thirteen rebounds. It was a grinding contest, a great tune-up for the rugged Big Ten schedule ahead.

A Painful Loss

A couple of days after the Florida State game, Jared received a text message from his biggest fan, offering advice: "Instead of always going for the charge, swipe at the shooter's hand." Jared smiled.

The message was from Uncle Brief, who was never shy about suggesting ways Jared could improve. Brief had been an All-American post player in high school and had led Woodrow Wilson High in Camden to a state championship in 1969. The team was coached by Gary Williams, who later led the University of Maryland to a national championship. Jared saved that message from Brief, not knowing it would be the last he'd ever receive from him.

Brief died of a heart attack the next day. He was 58. His death was a big blow to our family, especially to Jared. Jared and Brief spoke regularly, including before games. They had developed a special bond and Jared looked up to Brief. Brief never sugarcoated his advice to Jared, about basketball or life, and Jared respected it. He would miss Brief terribly.

Jared attended Brief's viewing a few days later and scored 40 points in a win over IUPUI that night. He dedicated his performance to Brief.

Finding His Way

Jared settled into a groove for the Buckeyes, continuing to soak up knowledge from his veteran teammates and Coach Matta and his staff. To be successful at anything, we must always stay aware of how much we don't know. Jared has always trusted himself on the court but constantly seeks to learn and improve. The Buckeyes rolled through the remainder of their non-conference games unscathed and opened their Big Ten schedule with a convincing win at Indiana on New Year's Eve. It was another total team effort by the Buckeyes, with four players scoring in double figures. The club was confident and unselfish, each player understanding his role in Coach Matta's scheme. The Buckeyes had multiple weapons, could attack you from inside or outside, and the club prided itself on its intensity. More than anything, they were hungry.

True to the nature of the Big Ten Conference, there are no easy nights, regardless who you're playing. That was especially true for unbeaten and second-ranked Ohio State. Following the victory over Indiana, the Buckeyes endured four consecutive nail-biters, winning each. It seemed a different player always stepped up for them, hitting a key three-pointer or clutch free throws or nabbing a steal or rebound in the waning moments. The players trusted each other and Coach Matta, and were finding a way to get it done in crunch time.

Jared was finding his way, too, and that included some frustration as a freshman learning the ropes in the Big Ten. Against Michigan, the Wolverines utilized a defense Jared hadn't seen before, double-teaming him from the baseline instead of the normal high side and cutting off his angles to the basket. Michigan defenders swarmed him in the paint. He had several turnovers in the game and fouled out late.

It was a rough night for him, but a valuable learning experience. Most importantly, the Buckeyes won the game. In the next game, against Penn State, the Nittany Lions helped off guard Aaron Craft to double-team Jared down low. This time, instead of getting frustrated, Jared kept kicking the ball back outside to an open Craft, who nailed several clutch three-pointers. Jared prides himself on his passing, on finding the open man. Craft's effective shooting opened things up for Jared to operate in the post.

Bitter Sweet Sixteen

The Buckeyes became the top-ranked team in the nation, making the bull's-eye on their backs even bigger. Against a ranked Illinois team on the road, the Buckeyes battled back from an eight-point second half deficit and again found a way to win, led by a couple of key three-pointers from freshman Deshaun Thomas, his first three-pointers in Big Ten action. Jared played the entire game, finishing with 27 points, 16 rebounds and 3 blocks. To Jared, personal stats have never mattered. It's all about winning.

Ohio State blew out 12th ranked Purdue at home, their most dominant performance of the season, and moved to 21-0. They were 24-0 entering a game at Wisconsin, where they suffered their first loss. The Buckeyes built a 15-point lead in the first half but squandered it, going cold down the stretch while Wisconsin was red-hot from three-point land. The focus for Ohio State, however, remained winning the Big Ten championship, and it was there for the taking.

The Buckeyes lost again at Purdue a week later, then righted the ship and stormed through the conference tournament, winning it and the Big Ten championship.

Ohio State entered the NCAA tournament as the top overall seed. The Buckeyes opened regional play in Cleveland, hammering UT-San Antonio and George Mason. Ohio State would face Kentucky in a Sweet Sixteen matchup. The week leading to the Kentucky game was an emotional one for Jared. The game was being played in Newark, New Jersey, not far from where his Uncle Brief led Woodrow Wilson High in Camden to that state championship. Brief would have savored a return to Jersey, would have been in the stands cheering for Jared and the Buckeyes to reach the Final Four.

Big Ten Tournament Champions, 2011.
(photo courtesy of Dispatch Printing Company)

For my sons, Brief was a treasured link between my dad and me. Brief attended many of their games over the years, rooting them on and yelling advice. Though I valued my relationship with him, the parallels in behavior between Brief and my dad were uncanny to me.

Like my dad, Brief had never held himself accountable in life. He bounced from relationship to relationship, scheme to scheme, looking for shortcuts to riches instead of buckling down and doing the work. Like my dad, when challenges arose in life, Brief cut and ran instead of facing them. He'd live at Mom Betty's house for a while, then move out, then move back home again. It was an endless cycle for him. At almost 60 years old, Brief was still living with his mom, still running back home when things got tough. My dad had done the same thing.

Brief was a smart man, but he refused to accept responsibility for his circumstances in life. He was volatile, always quick to anger about little things and to blame others. I tried to get him to calm down, to see things from a different perspective, to see the bigger picture and realize the things that bothered him so much wouldn't matter in a day or a month or a year. Sadly, he could never let it go. He died of a heart attack, just like my dad. Brief had grown up watching my dad's wayward behavior all those years and simply mirrored what he'd seen. Ironically, despite the pain I felt growing up without my dad around, when I saw how Brief behaved, I felt lucky I hadn't fallen into that trap. But I still loved my brother Brief.

For any of us, it's important to realize that we have a choice to get angry or remain calm when something doesn't go the way we planned. Just because someone else says or does something we don't like, it doesn't mean we have to fly off the handle. Getting angry or staying calm and keeping things in perspective is a choice we make. And given the emotional and physical toll anger takes on us, why not choose calmness instead? It's easier said than done, of course. It takes constant practice. But we must try to keep in mind that, ultimately, it's our choice.

Ohio State lost a heartbreaker to Kentucky in the Sweet Sixteen, 62-60, on a clutch shot by Brandon Knight with five seconds left. Kentucky played a swarming, physical defense and made things tough on Buckeye shooters all night. Ohio State ended the season 34-3.

Let the Money Chase You

Jared was named first team All-American and won the Wayman Tisdale Award as the National Freshman of the Year. He was also a finalist for the Wooden and Naismith Player of the Year Awards.

There was much speculation by fans and media about whether Jared would return to Ohio State for his sophomore season or bolt for expected lottery-pick riches in the NBA. There was talk among so-called experts that, if Jared entered the draft, he might be the first player chosen. Though many assumed Jared's exit to the NBA was imminent, the choice was a no-brainer for him and our family. He would return to Ohio State for his sophomore season.

Some people thought Jared was crazy to pass up the big bucks of an NBA lottery-pick contract, especially considering the risk of injury if he played another season in college. I understand those thoughts, because you never know about injuries. To our family, however, money has never been the most important thing. I always told my sons not to chase money when they grew up. I told them to work hard and focus and follow through at whatever they did. I believe if we stay focused on doing the work instead of seeking the reward, we'll eventually find that money is chasing us. We won't have to search for it. It'll find us. We'll look over our shoulder and there it'll be, hot on our trail.

Education has always been paramount in our family. I'm a teacher. Barbara is a teacher. Her mom was an educator. Our sons went to college. We believed another year at Ohio State would be a big plus for Jared. He was having a great time in school, was happy just being a kid and was in no hurry to give it up. We didn't see Jared as a "paycheck," didn't view his chance to play in the NBA as some sort of family meal ticket, so there was no urgency for him to turn pro. While each family's situation is different, I believe parents of youngsters in position to become pro athletes often focus too much on the money, overlooking what may be best physically and emotionally for the kids over the long term. I was convinced that, at 19, Jared wasn't ready to join the man's world that is professional basketball. The NBA is all about business, and if a player isn't ready emotionally, they are in for a rude awakening, on and off the court. Jared needed another season at Ohio State to get better as a player and grow as a person before he'd be ready to make the jump.

The bitter taste of losing to Kentucky in the Sweet Sixteen added fuel to Jared's competitive fire, and proved to be a great motivator for him to come back and try to help lead the Buckeyes to the Final Four. Though the team was losing the talent and leadership of Diebler and Lighty to graduation, much of its roster was returning along with Jared. Young players had gained valuable experience and understood now what it took to win a Big Ten championship and advance in the NCAA tournament. The players believed that if they kept improving, they could compete for a national championship.

Old Coaches Know When It's Time

While Jared had been settling into his first season at Ohio State, our Northland High team was focused on winning another state championship. Despite the losses of Jared and J.D. Weatherspoon to graduation, our other top players returned and our expectations were high. Our kids had learned the hard way from the loss to

Gahanna what humility means, had seen how letting their guard down and believing, even for a moment, the hype about being the best team in the nation had destroyed in the blink of an eye everything they'd worked for the previous season. They'd learned that making it to the top is easier than staying there, that the real work begins once you get there. And I had learned those lessons with them.

Among our returning players was Trey Burke, ranked as one of the top point guards in the country. Trey was a true leader and playmaker with supreme confidence. He could do it all.

We won our first fifteen games of the season, including a win over Akron St. Vincent-St. Mary, who would capture the Division II state championship that year. Our first defeat came at the hands of Lakewood St. Edward, in an 84-81 thriller. St. Ed's was a good team and had almost knocked off a few other ranked teams before beating us.

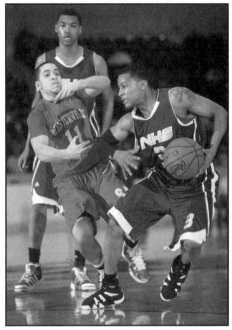

Trey Burke, doing what he did so well for our Northland High teams.
(photo courtesy of Dispatch Printing Company)

We won the rest of our regular season games and captured a record fifth straight City League Championship. The championship marked our 74th straight win in league play, spanning more than five years.

I announced my retirement as coach at Northland, effective at the end of the season, prior to the state tournament. It just felt like the right time for me. I'd been coaching at some level for nearly thirty years, had missed lots of special times with my family, including most of Jared's games during his freshman season at

Ohio State. I knew Jared would return for his sophomore year at Ohio State, and I'd get to see most of his games, even go on the road. We'd had a great run at Northland, especially those last five years, and I wanted to go out while we were on top. They say old coaches just know when it's time to hang it up, and I felt that time had come for me. I figured any added inspiration our players might draw from my decision to retire after the season would be a bonus heading into the tournament.

True to the competitive nature of the tourney, we took each opponent's best shot but kept advancing. We won a few blowouts and survived a few nail biters, including a rematch against Gahanna, by making key plays in crunch time. We made it to the state championship game but lost to Cincinnati LaSalle, 59-40. LaSalle was tenacious. Their players were in our faces early with intense defense, beating us on the boards and with backdoor cuts, and we didn't respond to the challenge. We were never in the game, and the blame fell to me. I did a poor job of coaching because our kids played tentatively. Any strategy adjustment I made in the game failed.

Intensity of the state high school tournament.
(photo courtesy of Dispatch Printing Company)

The loss proved a bitter end to what had been an emotional day for our Northland High family. Jared and the Buckeyes had been upset by Kentucky in the Sweet Sixteen the night before and we had attended the funeral of a team member's brother hours before our game. Losing the state championship game wasn't the way our senior players or I hoped to go out, of course, but LaSalle had performed brilliantly and deserved to win.

In the heat of crunch time, selfless teams come together.
(photo courtesy of Dispatch Printing Company)

It's Not about the X's and O's

I was grateful for the opportunity I'd had to coach at Northland High for a decade, to coach high school basketball for nearly twenty years, to work with so many wonderful kids who bought into our ideals and helped turn troubled programs around. Our kids had learned that being part of a team is about something bigger than any of us individually, that sharing in team glory is sweeter than any solo success we may enjoy. They had learned what accountability to ourselves and our teammates means, and understood the link between our actions away from the court and performance during crunch time on it. They had learned, sometimes through painful personal missteps, that it's not about winning ... it's about winning *the right way*, on the court and in life. They had learned that we play the game the way we live our lives.

I'm proud of the success we had at Northland, especially those last five years. In that span, we went 121-6, became the first public school ever to be ranked No. 1 in the *USA Today* poll, won five consecutive City League championships, played in two state championship games and won one. Most importantly, I'm proud that so many of our players through the years went on to college, many via scholarships, to obtain the education that is key to a successful life. The basketball, the athletics, is just a vehicle to help get kids to college.

Education has always mattered most to me. Whether teaching sociology or coaching over the years, I've considered it my duty to help kids make it to college and, more importantly, help them make it *through* college, supporting them as a friend or mentor or father figure after their playing days are done. Getting to college is a good start but, like in basketball, *finishing* is what matters. A college education prepares us to thrive during crunch time in life.

To me, coaching has never been about the X's and O's. After all, there are only so many plays any coach or team can utilize in the game of basketball, anyway. There's no play I could come up with as a coach that hasn't already been used in some fashion by another coach somewhere along the way. It's the young men *executing* those X's and O's who make all the difference because *we play the game the way we live our lives.*

My mission has been about trying to help mold those young men for success off the court, in the biggest game of all: life. At each of my stops along the way, I tried to do the right things for the right reasons, even when it meant sacrificing wins or possible additional championships. I was humbled and honored to coach a state championship team and win the Naismith National Coach of the Year Award. I wear the rings I received as a result of those blessings daily as a tribute to the players responsible for them, those kids who came together as One Heartbeat during crunch time to win big games. I wear the rings as a reminder of the power of playing with purpose, trust and togetherness to accomplish special things. I understand that none of it has ever been about me. For coaches, it should always be about our kids.

Are we doing our best each day to prepare players to succeed long after they've played their last game? Are we doing our best to help them understand the impact of their decisions and actions on others? Are we doing our best to help them realize what is possible in life when we put our ego aside and focus on helping our teammates to improve? Are we doing our best to help kids realize that consistent right effort and attitude can take us to incredible heights?

Regardless of our won/lost record as coaches, if our kids are going on to become leaders and live productive lives, we're winning. If they're contributing to society in a positive way and are becoming good fathers and husbands and neighbors and employees, we're winning. No matter how many games we win or lose, that's still the most important record of all.

Peaks, Valleys and a Final Four Run

Jared entered his sophomore season at Ohio State with lofty expectations for the team and himself. Though the Buckeyes had been ranked No. 1 and made it to the Sweet Sixteen the previous season, they had fallen short of contending for the national title. The way Jared and his teammates saw it, they still had unfinished business to take care of.

He had averaged a double-double as a freshman, had been named a first-team All-American, had won the Wayman Tisdale Award as the National Freshman of the Year, but continued to work hard on his game during the off-season, especially his outside shooting. Jared also worked harder on his conditioning, prepping himself to play either the four or five spot for the Buckeyes, wherever Coach Matta needed him. Jared toned his

Ya Gotta Finish!
(photo courtesy of Dispatch Printing Company)

body and lost nearly thirty pounds prior to his sophomore season.

Though the Buckeyes had lost the valuable leadership that David Lighty, John Diebler and Dallas Lauderdale provided, several key players returned. Coach Matta had landed another stellar recruiting class, too, and as Jared, Aaron Craft, Deshaun Thomas and company had done the previous year, those highly-touted freshmen would be expected to contribute immediately.

The Buckeyes started the season ranked in the top five, and rolled through their first few non-conference games. Then, seventh-ranked Florida visited Columbus. The Gators got off to a hot start in the game, but the Buckeyes turned up the heat on defense, forced a bunch of Florida turnovers, and won the game handily.

The second-ranked Buckeyes hosted third-ranked Duke in the Big Ten/ACC Challenge in late November, and the atmosphere in Value City Arena was electric. It was a special night for the Buckeyes. They scored the game's first eleven points and never looked back, storming to an 85-63 win. Jared had 21 points and Buford, Thomas and Craft were close behind. It was a total team effort for Ohio State.

Jared suffered back spasms in the Duke game that kept him out of a much-anticipated matchup at Kansas a couple of weeks later. The Buckeyes hung tough against the Jayhawks in legendary Allen Fieldhouse, one of the toughest places to play in the country, but fell, 78-67. The Buckeyes lost at Indiana on New Year's Eve, and again at Illinois the following week. The club temporarily struggled to find its footing as players adapted to their roles. They rattled off six wins in a row and then lost an ugly game at home to Michigan State, 58-48, succumbing to the rugged Spartan defense and their own questionable shot selection.

Ohio State's struggles continued a week later with a loss at Michigan, in which the Buckeyes again displayed suspect shot selection and, at times, appeared to be focused more on individual achievement than working together as One Heartbeat. They suffered their third loss in a five-game stretch against Wisconsin, showing inability to execute on offense and make stops down the stretch. With their hopes to win a third straight Big Ten championship hanging by a thread and questions about their willingness to play as a team instead of individuals lingering, the Buckeyes regrouped to win tense ballgames at Northwestern and Michigan State, clinching a share of the Big Ten championship. The Buckeyes lost to Michigan State in the championship game of the conference tournament.

Ohio State entered the NCAA tournament as a No. 2 seed. They dispatched Loyola (Maryland) and shone during crunch time in a tight game against Gonzaga to return to the Sweet Sixteen. They lost a big lead in the second half but took control down the stretch to beat Cincinnati, then defeated top-seeded Syracuse in a regional final slugfest to secure a berth in the Final Four in New Orleans.

Jared enjoys the heat of battle.
(photo courtesy of Dispatch Printing Company)

Seeing It Slip Away

The Buckeyes faced Kansas in a national semifinal, a rematch of their regular season contest. Jared had missed that game and looked forward to helping the Buckeyes against the Jayhawks this time around. The Buckeyes had overcome their share of adversity to reach the Final Four, most of it self-inflicted. Aside from Jared's back issues, the team had been forced to look at itself in the collective mirror, to realize the agendas and seeming selfishness that appeared to splinter the club late in the season must be wiped out if they hoped to make a run at a national title.

To the club's and Coach Matta's credit, they had turned it around in time to nab a share of a third consecutive Big Ten title and reach the Big Ten championship game. They had regained their togetherness, and their accountability to each other was again evident during those pressure-cooker tourney games leading to the Final Four.

Against Kansas, the Buckeyes started strong, jumping to a thirteen-point lead midway through the first half. They led by nine at halftime. In the second half, Kansas came out hot and the Buckeyes struggled to make shots, with no rhythm on offense. Ohio State hung tough, however, and the lead went back and forth. With a couple of minutes to go, it was anybody's game. But Kansas made the plays down the stretch, and held on for a 64-62 win.

While Kansas deserved credit for turning it around in the second half and doing what it took to win, the Buckeyes knew they'd let victory slip away. They had failed to finish, had veered from the togetherness it takes to win the banner games. Jared was named All-American for the second straight year, the first player in more than twenty years to be named All-American as a freshman and sophomore.

A Dream Realized and the Real Work Begins

A few days later, he announced his decision to enter the 2012 NBA draft. The obstacles he'd overcome during his sophomore season, especially emotionally, had prepared him for the rigors of the NBA, and he had continued to get physically stronger. The time was right for him to enter the draft. Jared had been forced to address his own immaturity during what was, at times, a trying season for the Buckeyes, and he persevered and came out stronger for it on the other side, capped by the team's Final Four appearance.

Jared loved his time at Ohio State and learned a lot from Coach Matta and his staff. It was an honor to our family that Jared got to play for Coach Matta, to follow his brother J.J. in contributing to the rich tradition of Buckeye basketball. Like J.J., Jared will always be a proud Buckeye. That goes for our whole family. As the NBA draft approached, there was concern by a few team doctors at the NBA draft combine about Jared's supposed back problems. These doctors issued a so-called "red flag" to their teams about Jared's back issues, suggesting it was too risky for those teams to pick him in the first round of the draft. Before the red flag was issued, Jared had been projected as a lottery pick, likely among the first ten players to be chosen in the draft.

The NBA is big business and there is huge money at stake for teams. Though our family was confident from additional testing he'd undergone that Jared's back was OK, those doctors had a job to do for their teams, and we respected that. They saw it the way they saw it. While the lingering uncertainty about his draft status was tough on Jared, he understood the doctors were obligated to their teams to be cautious.

The speculation about Jared's health snowballed, however, fueled in part by the inaccurate coverage of a few reporters focused only on being first to the finish line, regardless of their sloppiness. I have great respect for many sportswriters and reporters, but some seem to have lost their way amid the social media frenzy, overwhelmed by the immediacy of pushing a "send" button and buoyed by a sense of virtual reality bravado. Increasingly, it seems, some reporters try to inject themselves into a story, rather than simply reporting it, rolling the dice on their integrity in a rush to half-truths.

Regardless, our family knew that wherever Jared may be picked in the draft, it would be as God intended. And that was good enough for us.

As draft day neared, Jared slipped down the selection board. No longer projected as a lottery pick, he was not invited to New York City to attend the draft with other likely top picks. Instead, Jared hosted a draft party for family and friends at Eddie George's restaurant in Columbus. Jared saw it as a blessing to be able to share a special evening with those who'd supported him through the years.

Jared was selected by the Boston Celtics in the first round of the NBA draft, the 21st player chosen overall. The anxiety he had felt leading up to the draft faded instantly, replaced by excitement and anticipation. It was almost too good to be true. Not only had Jared realized his dream, a chance to play professional basketball, but he would have an opportunity to do it with the Celtics, the team that had won more championships than any other in NBA history. He would have an opportunity to learn from the best, from a championship coach in Doc Rivers and sure-fire Hall of Famers like Kevin Garnett and Paul Pierce. To Jared, it seemed a match made in Heaven. He had always been about winning, had always been happy to trade personal stats for team success, and now he was joining an organization that defined unselfishness. Jared knew that, despite all the work he'd done and success he'd enjoyed in basketball from grade school to high school, from AAU ball to

At Jared's Draft Party. A son's dream of playing professional basketball realized.
(photo courtesy of Dispatch Printing Company)

Ohio State, his real work was just beginning. God had blessed him with a dream realized and he planned to make the most of it.

Jared had little time to celebrate his selection by the Celtics, as he was soon headed to sites in Florida and Las Vegas to play for Boston's Summer League Team. NBA Summer League rosters typically include rookies, younger bench players and unsigned players. Summer League competition consists of a dozen or so games over a few weeks, and enables fans and media to get a look at top rookies in their earliest transition from college basketball to the NBA.

His solid performance in Summer League action reaffirmed the Celtics organization's belief in Jared's abilities. His toughness, solid positioning, strong rebounding and passing skills were on display in those games and, though it was only his small first taste of professional basketball, Summer League competition gave Jared a good feel for what it would take to perform well consistently in the NBA.

Solid Start, Abrupt End

Jared's role with the Celtics as the season started was to provide solid minutes off the bench, bringing a spark by banging inside and hitting the glass and playing solid defense and doing the dirty work he's comfortable doing in the post. Though Jared prides himself on his work ethic, having an opportunity to witness firsthand how hard veteran teammates like Kevin Garnett and Paul Pierce, for example—two of the NBA's all-time greats—continue to work, and the passion they bring and respect they give to the game, made a big impact on him. As a rookie, Jared

Jared was blessed to be drafted by the Boston Celtics, one of the winningest franchises in professional sports history. (photo courtesy of Getty Images Sport)

knew he was fortunate to have an opportunity to learn the game, including the mental approach to it, from guys like K.G. and Paul and Coach Doc Rivers.

The physical and mental learning curve necessary to become a consistent, productive NBA player is considerable and, early in the season, Jared found himself "thinking" a bit too much on the court, which blocked his natural physical feel for the game. Thinking too much causes a player to react more slowly. Jared was on "information overload," and it slowed him on the court a bit. It was important for him to realize that he couldn't possibly learn everything at once, that it would take some time to digest it all.

As Jared started to understand that it was a process, that it wasn't possible to absorb everything instantly, he began to relax his mind and let his feel for the game take over. He knew that, while he had much to learn, he could lean on those two important things each of us has control over: our effort and our attitude. As Jared began to "react" on the court instead of thinking so much, his physical ability to play the game fell in line and he started to find his comfort zone. On Christmas Day, Jared had his best game of the season, coming off the bench to score 16 points and grab 7 rebounds as the Celtics beat the Brooklyn Nets. Jared's confidence rose, and his performance followed. In January, he averaged 7 points and 7 rebounds in just over twenty minutes a game, and became a starter for the Celtics. The team was winning, and Jared was finding his way. He made his share of rookie mistakes, like picking up unnecessary fouls away from the ball by not knowing when to back off the physical contact. But he continued to learn and improve.

A few days after moving into the Celtics' starting lineup, Jared's season ended abruptly. He underwent lumbar disk surgery and would require several months to recover. It was a tough emotional blow for Jared, especially considering that he'd begun to contribute consistently for the team. I've always believed that God never gives us more than we can handle, and Jared quickly realized that the surgery and recovery was simply another obstacle for him to overcome on the journey to live his dream. He wasn't about to indulge in self-pity. Each of us will face obstacles on our life journey. Those obstacles may be mental, emotional or, as in Jared's case, physical; whether we overcome those obstacles is largely up to us. Remember: It's not about what happens to us in life, but how we choose to respond to what happens that matters most. Jared knew he had no control over his injury, but that he absolutely had control over his response to it, his attitude about it. Every cloud has a silver lining, as they say, and the way Jared saw it, if the injury were going to occur at all, at least it happened after he'd had the opportunity to prove to the Celtics he could play, that he belonged. He had earned the respect of his teammates, including leaders K.G. and Pierce, by working hard and staying humble and keeping a positive attitude, no matter his role.

The Celtics are a first-class organization and their support of Jared in dealing with his injury, surgery and rehabilitation was tremendous. Their belief in him as a person and player, and excitement about his future with the team, meant so much to Jared. Now, it was up to him to do his part to rehabilitate and come back strong for next season.

PART II

PART II

Introduction: The Values 'Starting Five'

In basketball, a team's starting five symbolizes the club's greatest strengths, each player filling a unique role to help the team succeed. Each starter brings something different to the game, some specialized skill that complements their teammates' abilities and contributes to the success of the whole. From the point guard to the shooting guard, from the small forward to the big forward to the post player, each starter must focus on filling their role within the team structure, working toward individual excellence while trusting their teammates to do the same, all sharing the common ground of commitment to the team's best interests.

It's the same with our core values in life. The key principles to which we subscribe should stand for our best, each bringing something unique and positive to our lives and the lives of others while working together to keep us and our team on a winning track.

The values "starting five" here represents the power I believe we possess to win every day by playing with purpose, by blowing past ego and overcoming adversity en route to raising our game and rising to our potential. These principles and their components have been gleaned from my experiences on and off the court, from transcending childhood turmoil to decades spent developing strong character in kids as a teacher and coach, from enduring painful personal loss to enjoying exhilarating team triumph, being married to the same woman for thirty years to raising three sons who became college athletes.

These principles comprise offense and defense rolled into one. Offensively, they attack bitterness and blame with attitude and effort, pushing intention up the court and scoring with follow-through. Defensively, they guard against selfishness and prevent mediocrity from penetrating our mindset. This "starting five" is tough in transition, too, there to help us rebound quickly from our mistakes and get back in position to succeed.

Sustained team success is difficult without depth, and it's crucial that we have solid bench players ready to spell our starters and provide a spark when necessary. In basketball and life, we must constantly adjust to the flow of the game and be able to call upon those supporting players and principles where needed. I'm convinced that our commitment to, and consistent practice of, these "starting five values," boosted by those role-playing principles coming off the bench, will put us in slam-dunk position to make a championship-level impact in life, no matter what the scoreboard says.

ACCOUNTABILITY

To succeed in life, nothing matters more than accountability, which means accepting unfailing ownership of our actions. No matter if we're at home, school, work, hanging out with friends or on a basketball court, each of us is responsible for what we say, think and do. Our willingness or reluctance to practice accountability in all areas of our lives, to make the right decisions for the right reasons, without excuses, will make the difference between success and failure: for us *and* for our team. We must not underestimate the impact our acceptance or avoidance of accountability has on the team as a whole. It can help lift the team to great heights, or destroy it.

Some players think accountability means doing just enough during practices or games to keep their teammates and coaches satisfied. But accountability stretches far beyond the court. It encompasses everything we do. If a player cares about accountability only where the game is concerned, they're in trouble. How does the player handle their business when the game ends or practice is over? There's no such thing as part-time accountability. If a player doesn't respect themselves or their teammates enough to be accountable off the court, they cannot be counted upon to deliver when crunch time comes, that crucial time near the end of a game when the outcome hangs in the balance. The player's family or friends or employer will not be able to count on them, either, when adversity arises and it's all on the line.

Accountability is essential. People must be able to rely on you, and you must be able to rely on *yourself.* Players who embrace accountability away from the game, who fulfill their duties without taking shortcuts, who seek ways to serve others, become prepared and confident. That preparedness and confidence will be on display during crunch time, and those players will rise to the challenge.

Championship teams are filled with players who embrace accountability. These players make selfless choices that have a positive impact on their families and teammates. That way, they aren't weighed down with the baggage of bad karma while playing the game. Their "emotional vision" on the court is clear, and they're free to rise in crunch time. They're able to perform best when it matters most.

Conversely, teams that always lose often include players who avoid accountability off the court. These players make selfish choices, care only about what's in it for them. They do as they please, regardless of the repercussions. They carry the burden of those bad choices and it sinks them when crunch time comes. Their carelessness away from the court infects their game, and they fold under pressure.

To me, it's simple: *We play the game the way we live our lives.* That means the way we handle our duties *off* the court dictates how we'll perform when the game is on the line. We can't separate the two. Karma won't let us. If we're doing what we're supposed to, without shortcuts, we'll be confident and in control when crunch time comes. We'll thrive when the pressure is on, because accountability will be normal to us. But players who avoid responsibility will shrink during crunch time. Because life consists of those crunch time moments. If we've done the work and we're prepared, we'll come through in the clutch. Because you play the game the way you live your life.

Three Yeses

I believe accountability for each of us means always being able to answer "yes" to the following:

1. **Are we *where we're supposed to be* (at a given time of day, per our responsibilities)?**

2. **Are we there *when we're supposed to be there* (not showing up late or skipping out early)?**

3. **Are we doing *what we're supposed to be doing* (giving it our best) while there?**

If we can consistently answer "yes" to each question, we're on track for success in life. I call it the *Three Yeses*. It seems simple, perhaps, but if we can't answer yes to each, there's a problem waiting to happen.

Being *where we're supposed to be* lays the foundation for good things to happen for us in life. It's the essential first step toward putting ourselves in position to succeed. Sometimes the "where" is spelled out clearly, like being at school or work or sports practice. If we're students, for example, we know we're supposed to be in school during the day. If we decide not to go, we're pulling away the foundation from which good things can be built. If we refuse that fundamental first step, we're creating our own obstacles to success. If we choose to miss work because we don't like the boss or the weather is nice or we want to hang out with our friends instead, we're blocking our own path to progress.

Being somewhere *when we're supposed to be there* signifies maturity, acknowledges that, though we may be having a bad day or it may be inconvenient for us, we're committed to our obligations and those who are counting on us. We don't slip in to work or school or practice a few minutes late, or angle for an early exit. Showing up early or staying beyond the minimum shows purpose and commitment to improvement, says we're interested in more than mediocrity. Being great requires great sacrifice no matter how talented we may be. It didn't matter to Michael Jordan when practice started or ended each day. He was still going to work hard on his own to get better. He was committed to excellence.

Doing what we're supposed to be doing (consistently giving our best) brings it all together for us. Leading with optimum effort says we're serious about making special things happen for ourselves, and we won't accept average. While the first two Yeses lay the foundation for success, this one is the difference-maker. If we're just going through the motions and not giving our best, we're wasting ourselves. We're not wasting time, because we don't own time. We can't control that sun rising and setting each day. All we can do is maximize the moments in between. If we let them pass us by, we're wasting *ourselves*. If we clown around in class, for example, refuse to pay attention or try to learn anything while there, that clock on the wall keeps ticking. If the class lasts an hour, that hour will tick away whether we try to better ourselves or not. If we've made the effort to show up in the first place, why not try to learn and improve while we're there? Why not make the most of those valuable moments God gives us? The only way to do it is by holding ourselves accountable.

Accountability requires self-discipline. Self-discipline means *listening to ourselves and not talking back*, means following through on what we know have to do, even if we're tempted to push it aside and do something else. Being accountable doesn't mean we can't have fun; far from it. But having fun means more when we've done the work we're supposed to do, *when* we're supposed to do it, the *way* we're supposed to do it. Playing golf is one of my favorite things to do, for example, but I wouldn't be able to enjoy it if I were ignoring my responsibilities.

Winners make the most of each moment by holding themselves accountable, by being *where* they're supposed to be, *when* they're supposed to be there, and *doing* what they're supposed to be doing with optimum effort. Three Yeses.

One Heartbeat

As a coach, I believe accountability to the team means applying the same set of rules, or guidelines, to the whole squad, with no exceptions made for the best players. I'm not referring to how coaches deal with players one-on-one because that may be influenced by individual circumstances, issues the player may be facing off the court, etc. There are numerous factors that affect a coach's one-on-one approach to players. Players come from different backgrounds, different family situations, face unique challenges, and coaches should adjust their approach accordingly.

But, where the team as a whole and its mission to succeed is concerned, it's crucial that coaches insist on accountability by each player to the group and identify and eliminate individual agendas from the start. Coaches must make it clear to players that, no matter how talented they may be, they are pieces of a larger puzzle, a part of something *bigger than themselves*, and none is exempt from the expectations of the whole. Bad decision-making by one player can undo the best efforts of the team. If a coach has one set of guidelines for a star player and another for the other players, the meaning of that message is lost.

I believe in a *One Heartbeat* approach, which means all of us, coaches and players alike, are working in synergy with shared expectation, all part of the same body and dependent on each other, all pulling in one direction to put the team in the best position for success.

Exceptions a coach makes to the *One Heartbeat* approach, like treating star players differently, causes that single, unified team "heartbeat" to splinter into three weaker ones, each with a different rhythm, each sapping the team's collective strength, eventually killing the team's chance to succeed.

Those three weaker heartbeats consist of:

1. **A group of players who side with the star player when conflict arises, who are afraid of being at odds with the star player;**

2. **Another group of players who resent the special treatment being given the star player by the coach;**

3. **A third group of players who hang in limbo, somewhere in the middle, seeking to avoid conflict with the other two groups. If a coach permits a culture that allows such splintering to occur, the odds of the team winning the "banner games," as I call them, the biggest games, become slim. The team may still win it share of games, but when crunch time comes in the biggest games, when the lights are brightest, those three weaker heartbeats will sap the club's strength. Teams can win the banner games only when coaches and players are working in synergy, with singular focus, all part of *One Heartbeat*.**

Walking the Talk

Several times in my coaching career, my belief in a *One Heartbeat* team approach has been tested, and each time proved to be a defining moment for me. The first time, early in my career as a coach at East High School in Columbus, when a star player showed up late and expected to board the bus for a road game, I knew it was an opportunity to demonstrate that what I'd been preaching to the team wasn't just talk. I refused to let him board the bus and later, after he'd found alternative transportation to the game, I didn't let him play. We lost the game that night with our star player sitting on the bench. However, he was never late again and that incident brought our team closer together.

A similar situation occurred while I was coaching at Beechcroft High School in Columbus. When our star player, a first-team All-Ohio player, missed practice the day before a big game, I didn't let him play in a game that would decide the division championship. Despite pressure from his father, I didn't waver, and the team was the better for it.

My belief in adherence to a *One Heartbeat* team approach hit painfully close to home for me during the 2007-08 state tournament when, as I mentioned earlier, I had to suspend my son Jared for a key game because he'd been slacking off on his schoolwork and had refused to hold himself accountable for it. Our previously-undefeated Northland High team lost the game, ending our season in bitter fashion, and Jared learned a valuable lesson about accountability and the impact our choices, on and off the court, has on our teammates. Simply being a talented player means nothing if we're not making the right decisions in life, if we're cheating ourselves and our team. Ultimately, our poor decision-making will cost us, often when it matters most. That lesson, tough as it was for him to understand at the time, proved valuable to Jared. It helped to make him a better student and player. He had learned that accountability is about doing the right things, for the right reasons, consistently, without excuses. It helped him realize that winning or losing in life isn't just about what happens on the basketball court. As members of a team, we're all a part of something bigger than ourselves, all part of *One Heartbeat*.

Maximizing the Moment

As I said, it's impossible for us to waste time, because we don't *own* time. None of us can control that sun rising and setting each day. If we're not making the most of the precious moments God gives us to become better, we're wasting *ourselves* instead.

To reach our potential, we must learn to *maximize the moment*, to understand that the only time we have is *now*, this moment. No matter our age, no matter how much time we may think we have to make our dreams come true, it won't happen unless we're *maximizing the moment*. It starts with the seconds. Because seconds become minutes, and minutes become hours, and hours become days, become months, become years, in a blink. It snowballs quickly. If we waste the moments God gives us, our dreams will never happen.

Playing golf has taught me the value of *maximizing the moment*, of realizing that, regardless whether the last shot I hit was good or bad, the only shot that matters is the one in front of me, the one I'm about to hit *in this moment*. It's the only shot I can do anything about. If I'm still thinking about the previous shot, or the shots to come, it steals my focus. It wastes the moment. It's the same in basketball. It's the same in life.

I always encourage players to focus on *maximizing the moment*, especially during crunch time of games, when the outcome hangs in the balance. I try to help them understand that the next play, or the next shot, is the only one we can control.

During one contest, we led by a point with seven seconds to go in the game. One of our players made a bad pass, giving our opponent the ball and a chance to win. I called timeout. In the huddle, I asked our players a simple question. "Fellas," I asked, "Would you rather be *ahead* by a point and playing defense with seven seconds left to close out the game, like you are, or be *trailing* by a point but have the ball?" They responded in unison. "Playing defense!"

"Well, then, you're right where you want to be," I told them. Our players were calm and focused. They weren't about to melt down emotionally worrying about what might happen as a result of our turnover. They had already put it out of their minds, knew it was useless to waste a second of energy dwelling on it because they couldn't change it. It was already in the past. They were focused on the only thing that mattered, which was the next play and those last seven seconds of the game. It was all about handling their business *in that moment*. They played strong defense, contested the other team's shot, and we won the game.

It's important we keep our focus on the only shot we can control, which is the one right in front of us. It's called *maximizing the moment*.

EFFORT AND ATTITUDE

Two Things We Can Always Control

We can't control everything that happens to us in our lives, and adversity is part of the game. But no matter the challenge, there are two things we can control that have everything to do with our ability to succeed: one is our *effort*, and the other is our *attitude*.

Effort and attitude are inseparable, for good or bad. Players who have a positive attitude, for example, always give great effort, also. In the same way, players with poor attitudes usually have crummy work habits, too. Effort and attitude go hand-in-hand, and will make or break a player and team, no matter how talented that player or team may be.

Talent alone does not ensure success; far from it. We've all seen talented athletes who fail because of poor effort and attitude. Bad attitude and effort stem from selfishness, from an ego-based, "What's in it for me?" mindset.

From a team perspective, effort and attitude make the difference between champions and also-rans. We see it constantly: teams loaded with talented players who lack work ethic and positive attitude, mistakenly convinced they can win with talent alone. These teams may still win some games, but will lose the ones that matter most. Because *talent can take us places poor character can't sustain*. That means no matter how talented a player may be, no matter how high the player may rise, poor character will inevitably drag them down.

Players who try to sneak by on talent alone may fool themselves, but they can't fool their teammates or coaches, at least not for very long. Players who avoid the hard work of improvement, who ignore commitment to their teammates, are eventually exposed.

Pat Penn, my coach at Oberlin University, called the process of uncovering a player's attitude and effort level *eliminating the bushes*, which means chopping away excuses the player may be using to hide from commitment. When the excuses are gone, when there are no more "bushes" left for a player to hide behind, the player has a choice: either buy in, become accountable and commit, or quit. It's a coach's duty to eliminate those bushes. From there, players with suspect attitude and effort fall away.

Displaying great attitude and effort doesn't mean we won't make our share of mistakes along the way. Mistakes happen. But they're easier to accept if we're giving our best and playing the game the right way.

We sometimes hear the terms "mental mistake" or "physical mistake" from sports broadcasters when describing player errors in games. With few exceptions, mental mistakes equal not playing as hard as we should, or that our attitude is lacking a bit. Mental mistakes mean we're not *where* we're supposed to be, *when* we're supposed to be there, *doing* what we're supposed to be doing. On the court, for example, it means we're not rotating to the basket properly on defense and we're giving up easy points because of it.

Physical mistakes, however, happen mostly as a result of playing hard. Playing hard means our effort and attitude is where it should be. If we're charging up the court with the ball on a fast break and we happen to dribble it off our foot, for example, that's a physical mistake. We were playing hard, were where we were supposed to be, doing what we were supposed to be doing, and we erred while hustling. It happens sometimes. But it's those avoidable mental mistakes that hurt the most and often cost us the game.

I used to tell my players they could make all the mistakes they wanted, as long as those mistakes happened while they were playing their hardest. While we hope the mistakes our players make are minimal, of course, we know they will happen. When they do, it's our job as coaches to encourage the players, not chastise them, to help them understand how the mistake happened and see how they may avoid it in the future.

There's no excuse for falling mentally asleep, for going through the motions with a ho-hum attitude. Attitude is everything. I'd rather coach a team that loses a game while playing with great attitude and effort than one that wins a game with lackluster effort any day.

As a parent, if faced with the choice, I'd rather see a kid bring home a report card showing an average grade but high marks for effort than one showing a good grade but low marks for effort. The effort and attitude are most important.

On the court, if we happen to make a bad pass and throw the ball away, fine. But we can't sulk about it. We have to hustle down the court on defense and try to get the ball back! We can't turn one error into two by failing to get back on defense and contesting what may seem like an easy shot for the other team. We can't assume they'll automatically convert that layup or bunny shot, because nothing is certain. We have to get back down the court on defense as quickly as we can, because our opponent might blow that easy shot and the rebound we snare by hustling back after our mistake may make a difference in the game. Great effort and attitude don't give up when they make a mistake. They keep coming.

Problem Players Can Run, but They Can't Hide Anymore

The power of social media today, of lightning-quick information travel, means player missteps, especially off the court, can be globalized instantly. As such, players are under a more powerful microscope than ever, scrutinized for even the smallest of transgressions. Players must understand this and hold themselves accountable. They must avoid putting themselves in places or situations that call their character into question.

In our society, big-time players, especially at the professional level, are placed on a pedestal by fans, who think those players can do no wrong. Many of those fans are kids who hope to grow up to be just like their favorite players someday. I believe athletes, whether they like it or not, are indeed role models and have a responsibility to represent their organizations, their schools, their communities, in a positive way. They owe it to their fans to be gracious and respectful.

The word "fan" comes from *fanatic*, of course, and we all know there are a few overzealous idiots out there who operate without rhyme or reason, who take their fandom beyond a point of return, crossing into unacceptable territory where confronting players or causing problems is concerned. Unfortunately, that's just the way it is. But the overwhelming majority of fans are committed to supporting their teams in a positive way, and players owe those fans excellent attitude and effort each time they take the floor. Players must make sound decisions off the court, too, realizing that their actions, either positive or negative, impact countless others who are counting on them.

Athletes who accept endorsement deals while refusing to embrace role model responsibility are operating in a disappointing gray area, happy to take the money they receive from their endorsement deals but conveniently turning the other cheek where showing gratitude or respect for the fans who root for them is concerned.

Increasingly, fans have grown weary of player behavioral missteps and are less inclined than ever to accept them, no matter how talented the player may be. Fans are resistant to giving players a pass for poor behavior anymore just because those players may score a lot of points or grab a bunch of rebounds each night. More than ever, fans have made it clear they expect quality character to accompany that player talent now. Talent alone is no longer enough.

And teams are getting that message from their fans. Slowly but surely, organizations are owning up to their obligation to fans to try to *win the right way*, with talented players who also possess good character. Teams that try to do otherwise will pay a heavy price, financially and from a public relations perspective, because fans are balking at supporting players (see: buying tickets, merchandise, etc.) who act out and embarrass the organization. Teams at the college and pro level are being held accountable by fans for the character of players they sign. Organizations are quicker to cut ties now with players who screw up, especially repeatedly, who disrespect the university or organization and fans and the game itself with their bad behavior. Big time sports is about branding and massive sums of money, and these organizations can no longer afford the public relations problems and considerable financial fallout players with poor character cause, no matter how talented those players.

Second chances still exist for players who make mistakes and accept the blame and commit to changing their ways for the long haul. But the opening is narrower now, and that window of opportunity is quicker to slam shut for good. Fans and teams are locked-in on player character, and their tolerance level for player missteps is low. Players must respect the game and make the right decisions off the court to make the most of their career, no matter their talent level. They may be able to get away with disrespecting the game for a little while, but the karma of the game will eventually catch up with them and deal them the hand they deserve. Karma won't allow them to violate the pure spirit of sport for long.

America Won't Let Us Fail (if we're doing the work)

When we're struggling, it's easy to feel sorry for ourselves, to fall into the self-pity trap and blame others for our troubles. It's called "playing the victim," and it leads to defeat. No matter what we're facing, if we keep a positive attitude and continue to give great effort, things will find a way of working out for us. We may not see the light at the end of the tunnel right away, but if we keep digging, sooner or later, it'll shine. In the meantime, we must keep digging and trust the process.

Our society faces enormous challenges, and many of them involve emotionally-charged issues for us. We rush to support this side or that for one reason or another, and entrench ourselves in our opinion. It's OK to have ideas about how things could be better, to express those views in the proper forum if we wish, but we can't let ourselves be consumed by the bitterness of a "victim" mindset.

Some people believe our lives are completely controlled by a select few, think the so-called "powerful people" at the top decide what happens to the rest of us, and can keep us from accomplishing special things. These people think there's no use in trying. They're quick to give up when adversity arises, to point fingers and find excuses and take a seat on the bench. They thrive on playing the blame game. But whenever we point a finger of blame at others, three fingers on that hand are pointing back at us. Instead of wasting our energy complaining, why not use it to improve our game?

Rather than fretting over things we can't control, why not focus on two things we can *always* control: our effort and attitude? If those are in the right place, then no matter what we face, our chances for success are strong. If we're working hard without excuses, respecting the game and trusting the process, good things will happen for us. If we're doing our part, America will not let us fail. With the right attitude and effort, we'll win all the games we're expected to win and emerge victorious from some games we probably should have lost. And when we taste defeat, we'll know we gave it everything we had, and credit our opponent for simply being better.

It's the same way in basketball. A player might not be the flashiest or most talented, but if they are smart, know where they're supposed to be on the court, when they're supposed to be there and what to do when they get there, are *efficient with their effort*— know how to make that effort count—they have a great chance to be successful. Making our effort count means putting ourselves in position for good things to happen, means being an effective "position player." Tim Duncan of the San Antonio Spurs is a great example. He's never been the flashiest guy on the court, won't overwhelm anyone with sheer athletic ability, but there's nobody better at making his effort count. He doesn't waste energy. He is a master at putting himself in position for opportunity. His so-called *basketball I.Q.* (which, essentially, equates to being the "coach on the court," a player with great understanding of how the game works and an ability to apply that understanding to performance to lift his teammates) is off the charts. My son Jared has never been the best pure athlete on the court, never been able to run the fastest or jump the highest, but is learning how to put himself in position for opportunity, and to make the most of that opportunity when he gets it. On defense, for instance, he's willing to take those tough charges, to dig for ball deflections, knows how to block out effectively to secure rebounds. He's not a high flyer in terms of leaping ability like some players, but he knows where he's supposed to be around the basket and what to do when he gets there. Jared is "effort efficient." He makes his use of energy count. There will often be players with more *skill* than we have, but if they're wasting effort, are unable to make their *energy* count, we'll prevail most of the time.

In life, we succeed by first putting ourselves *in position*, then knowing what to do when we get there. That doesn't mean success will come easily, or exactly when we expect it. It doesn't work that way. If success were easy, it would be hollow. There are no shortcuts or guarantees. We will face adversity on our journey, and the surest way to overcome it is with positive attitude and effort. People who claim they can't catch a break, that others are always blocking their path to success, are really victims of themselves, at the mercy of their own bad attitude and effort.

It goes back to those Three Yeses: Are we *where we're supposed to be* (to handle our responsibilities), *when we're supposed to be there* (arriving on time, not cutting out early), *doing what we're supposed to be doing* (to the best of our ability, consistently) while there? If so, somebody in position to help us achieve our dreams will spot our effort and become interested in seeing us succeed. That doesn't mean they'll do the work for us, but will be attracted to our work ethic and attitude and will likely lend a helping hand.

Passion is a trait shared by successful people, and it's contagious. Successful people enjoy helping others who are determined to succeed, who are giving their best instead of grasping for excuses. Someone out there is looking to help us succeed, but we must be willing to help ourselves first. Attitude and effort are *everyday things*. If they're in the right place, we can't go wrong, and we sure won't fail. America won't let us.

Participate in Your Own Dream

If we have a dream, we must work hard to make it happen. The embrace or avoidance of that effort is the difference between those who reach their personal mountaintop and those who don't. We all want to be successful, but simply wanting success isn't enough; we must *take action*. It's easy to talk about our talents or our great ideas or how we think we're a better player than so-and-so, but it takes discipline and desire and commitment to get it done. Some people are allergic to hard work; they'd rather try to take a free ride to the mountaintop on someone else's coattails instead. These people want a piece of the "gold dust" without earning it. They'd rather hitch their dream to someone else's hard-earned success.

It's foolish to expect that others will hand-deliver our dream for us. It's a waste of valuable time to sit around and hope someone comes to our dream rescue. It's up to us to climb that mountain … no excuses, no blame.

We're responsible for *participating in our own dream*, for putting in the effort necessary to achieve it. After all, if we refuse to help ourselves, if we don't believe we're worth giving our own best effort, why should anyone else believe it? Some folks feel they're entitled to success without working for it and slog through life lugging that troublesome sense of entitlement. They *wish* for things to happen, expect others to do the work on their behalf, instead of rolling up their sleeves and *making* them happen. We may believe in our dream, but we must plant the seeds. If we don't, we're cheating ourselves by settling for less than our best. Talk is cheap. We must act. What's the old adage? "Your actions speak so loudly, I can't hear what you say." That says it all.

Success means action. *Our dreams are within our own reality, so why not rise to meet them?* If we won't do the work necessary to realize our dream, we don't deserve to succeed. Some people make a habit of "wanting" from others, and their constant asking takes the place of doing. They talk about their dreams and take shots at the hopes of others. They expect others to help them make their dreams come true but they never help themselves. When they don't get what they ask for, when they ask for it, they give up and move on to their next illusion.

I call it the *Give Me, Lend Me, Can You Spare* Syndrome, and it's an endless cycle for these people. They straggle from relationship to relationship, destroying each by wanting from others without commitment to themselves. People caught up in the *Give*

Me, Lend Me, Can You Spare Syndrome burn these relationship
bridges when they become frustrated instead of expending the
effort to improve their circumstances. We all want to succeed, of
course, but we first have to put ourselves *in position* for success.
It happens by working, not wishing. If we trust ourselves and
keep working toward our dreams, making sure that our effort
matches our desire, we won't need anyone else's help. Because, in
the words of the great coach and leader Pat Riley, we'll find that
everything due us will arrive in the jet streams of our hard work.

Patience Makes the Crunch Time Difference

Action is key to making our dreams come true. We can't sit
around and wait on someone to hand-deliver our dreams for us.
We must continue to trust our vision and support that belief with
relentless effort each day. If we rely on tenacity alone, however,
we'll blow right through those strategic "slow down" signs along
the way and make the crucial turnover that wrecks our
championship chances.

In this warp speed world, our tendency is to *attack and keep
attacking*, to hurry up, to go faster and get things done quickly so
we can do more. But our aggression, if uncontrolled, will cost us
when crunch time comes. In those tense moments when the
game's outcome hangs in the balance, *patience* is the most valuable
player on the floor.

Some people just grab the ball and go every chance they get,
charging up the court on every possession, oblivious to their
teammates in a rush to the bucket. *Gotta get mine!*, they think.
But their haste often makes waste. In their hurry to score ego
points, they get sloppy, turning the ball over by dribbling it off
their foot or slamming recklessly into a well-positioned defender.
It's OK to be eager, but our eagerness must be tempered with
discipline and patience, especially during crunch time. We must

be able to slow ourselves down, especially mentally, when it matters most, to stay calm and make those key possessions count and put ourselves in the best position to win. Staying calm is difficult to do if we're scrambling all the time.

Being patient doesn't mean we can't go fast, or that we shouldn't stay aggressive. It means making sure we're not in *emotional overdrive*, out of control, playing sloppy and putting ourselves and our teammates in a bad position. It means we can hurry, but not rush.

When crunch time comes, when the spotlight is brightest, our character is uncovered. What we're really made of comes out. And that's where patience comes in. Patience stems from confidence, from knowing we've done the work and prepared ourselves the best we can and have earned the right to win.

Things move so quickly nowadays that it's easy to get swept up, to expend all our energy running here and there and not really accomplishing anything. Patience means slowing down to catch our breath, to assess where we are and prepare for where we're headed. It allows us to appreciate what we have, instead of always seeking more. Patience helps us realize that, while God may not always give us what we want, when we want it, one way or another he always gives us what we *need*. And there's a calmness that comes with that realization.

When I began coaching, I didn't understand that. I thought I controlled the time table, thought I could force things. I assumed that, just because I believed I was ready to become a head coach, God would instantly lay a job in my lap. It didn't happen that way. When I finally got my first high school head coaching job at East, I realized how much I'd learned in the meantime to better prepare me to handle those duties.

From a competitive standpoint, patience is essential to putting away our opponents. We've all seen games where a team leading by a sizable margin with a few minutes to go squanders that lead and loses the game. While the team that was trailing deserves credit for their comeback, of course, it happens largely because players on the team with the lead become *impatient*. They stop playing the *game* (executing the fundamentals that put them in position to win) and start playing the *scoreboard* (taking quick, questionable shots to pad their personal stats or committing silly fouls or taking possessions off). Their impatience is rooted in selfishness. And it costs them.

Aggression may get us *to* crunch time, but patience will carry us *through* it. Patience during crunch time doesn't mean being *passive*; it means being *purposeful*, staying committed to our teammates and continuing to do the things we've done successfully to establish that lead. Patience during crunch time will prove the difference between putting our opponents away or opening the door and allowing them to get back in the game.

Living in a Mansion but Thinking from the Street Corner

We've all seen the financial horror stories of millionaire athletes who blow their fortunes and go broke. We've all shaken our heads in figurative disgust wondering how in the heck they allow it to happen, convinced that if *we* were in their position, instead, we'd do things differently. While the specific details of these cautionary tales may differ somewhat, I believe the common-ground bottom line to most of them is a *lack of patience*.

With few exceptions, athletes and others who churn through huge sums of money until there's nothing left suffer from impatience, from a *want-it-all-right-now-and-don't-care-what-it-costs* mentality. They're in a hurry to prove to themselves and the world that they've arrived, and that haste costs them terribly. Instead of being patient and taking it a step at a time to lay the foundation for even bigger long-term financial success, they rush to show the world what they have *now,* their future financial security be damned.

Many of these players fall victim to a lethal combination of limited education and looking to please hangers-on from the old neighborhood who are hungry for dollar sign crumbs. Many of these players go to bed one night with no money at all to their names, and awaken the morning after signing a professional contract to an overflowing bank account. They grow up in poverty and are suddenly being handed the keys to the castle. It's instant, drastic change, and they're unprepared to handle it.

There are plenty of professional scam artists out there who specialize in preying on uneducated people with money and, unfortunately, wealthy young athletes are often among the easiest targets. They're easy targets mostly because they're *impatient*, because they're quick to buy the latest, greatest investment idea line from these financial predators, no matter how ridiculous the idea may be. Sadly, the players give now and pay dearly later. They refuse to move slowly and steadily instead, and it costs them.

In their impatience, these players race to accumulate "things" and show them off to the world at the first chance they get. Sadly, they attach their self-worth to the cars and jewelry and mansions they buy, spending like crazy to prove to others that they're somehow "better than." They succumb to the Big Business Marketing Machine, believing they *need* that $200,000 car or $2 million home to be happy. But no matter how many fancy cars or big houses or diamond necklaces they buy, they can't fill that void of self-worth. It has to be filled from within themselves.

These players are in warp-speed spending mode, but their education is still stuck in neutral. They may be living in a mansion, but their mindset is still back there on the street corner. Their financial situation may be different, but their thinking hasn't changed. They're still coming from a place of mental poverty.

What's wrong with waiting until we've saved enough money to secure our financial future to start spending, with obtaining those "things" after we've actually done the work? What's wrong with taking the slower and steadier route? If these players would exercise some restraint at the outset, focus on finding the right people to guide them through setting up budgets and savings plans, there would be plenty of time for spending money later … after the work is done, when they have matured in their thinking and approach to life.

While it's tough for players who suddenly have lots of money at their disposal, especially players who come from a life of poverty, to know exactly what to do, it's unacceptable for them to use their limited education as an excuse to let it all slip away. It's incumbent upon them to hold themselves accountable, to acknowledge their inexperience at handling money and put the brakes on their spending and find someone they can trust and who is qualified to help them avoid squandering their good fortune. Too often, however, they defer to those hangers-on from the old neighborhood, to those so-called friends or long-lost relatives who come out of the woodwork with their expectant *Where's mine?* mentality, who somehow feel entitled to a bit of that gold dust they did nothing to help create. These players become surrounded by hangers-on looking for a handout, and they give in to the pressure. They're more concerned with spending money and making those hangers-on happy today than pausing to consider what might happen tomorrow. It's impatience. And it can be overcome with the right mindset.

You Can't Buy Character (or Purpose)

In our society, there's a tendency to believe money solves everything, that it makes our problems disappear. But we see examples every day of wealthy people who self-destruct. Why? Because money can't buy good character! It can't tell right from wrong or make us respect the game or ourselves or our teammates. Money can be a wonderful byproduct of our passion, of living with purpose, and, if used wisely, can make a positive difference in our lives and the lives of others. There's nothing wrong with wanting to maximize our earning potential, and we have to provide for our loved ones. None of us wants to be poor. But if the pursuit of money is our sole focus in life, if we put it on a pedestal above family and integrity and teamwork, above doing the right things for the right reasons in an endless search for an extra buck, we're in for a troubled ride.

Countless mansions have been obtained at the expense of crucial family relationships, including priceless ones with our children. Tossing money or material things at kids can't replace the value of spending time with them. Our time is the most important gift we can give to anyone, especially our kids. We can send them to the best prep schools, can buy expensive cars and clothes for them, can make sure they never want for any material thing, but it can never compare to being there for them when they need us.

I believe our kids are like blank checks when they're born, and it's our duty as parents to help fill in those numbers for them as they grow, to help them understand their value in the world. We can't *buy* self-worth for them; it must be built by hand. And that takes time. It takes *being there*.

I know plenty of people, who, on the surface, seem to have it all. They have lots of material things ... big houses, fancy cars, expensive shoes, the

All in the family.
(photo courtesy of Dispatch Printing Company)

latest and greatest. But they're not happy. There's emptiness inside them that material things can't fill. Buying the best "stuff" might make them believe they're happy, might fill that void for a while, but it never lasts. Because it's not real. True happiness means opening the door at home and being grateful for *who is inside,* not *what's inside*, being thankful for our family members and teammates. That's where happiness resides. If we care only about money, we'll become slaves to it. We'll chase it anywhere. What about the currency of our relationships with loved ones? What about maximizing that value? Living only for money costs us the things that matter most.

In sports, especially at the professional level, there are plenty of players and coaches who are focused solely on chasing money. They're easy to identify; they move from job to job, team to team, pursuing those dollar signs with no interest in *purpose*, in helping to make their teammates or players better or becoming a part of something lasting, something bigger than themselves. All they care about is their next payday. To them, it's always all about *them*. And most of the time, they wind up miserable because of it. Why? Because greed is a magnet to further greed; players or coaches who are in it just for the money attract others of like mind. *Birds of a feather flock together*, as the old saying goes. Few of them are interested in making the commitment necessary to ultimate team success, and none of them benefit from their relationships of convenience. Rather than staying put somewhere and doing the heavy lifting necessary to develop team synergy, which leads to consistent winning, they continue hopping from job to job, getting in and out for the quick buck and avoiding real commitment. They play or coach well enough to get their dollars, but are usually stuck on the treadmill of team mediocrity.

Again, there's nothing wrong with wanting to make the most of our earning potential, especially in a profession with a smaller time window. But if we're using the gifts God gives us to help our teammates get better, to support the skills that support ours, are playing with purpose instead of only for ourselves and our bank account, we'll always come out on top in the end. Our talent will flourish within the team concept, the team will win, and we'll be paid well because of it. What's not to like about that picture?

When my sons were growing up, I always stressed to them the importance of not chasing money when they got older. I told them I believe if we just stay focused on doing the best job we can, on using our talents to help others improve without looking for rewards, sooner or later we'll look over our shoulders and see that money chasing us, instead of the other way around. It's a better option because we won't have to sell our souls or sell out our loved ones to get there. If we trust the process and keep doing our best work, we won't have to worry … the rewards will find us.

Greatest Threat to Excellence

I've often wondered why some people are satisfied with being less than their best in life. After all, what could be more rewarding for us than reaching our potential, than making maximum use of our God-given gifts? Somewhere along the way, it seems, simply being *good* at something—as an athlete or businessperson, as a parent or teacher or student—has become *good enough* to many, even where the potential for excellence exists.

In fact, I'm convinced the greatest threat to excellence today is simply being *good*. Why? Because being good seems safe. Plenty of folks will make the effort to upgrade from poor to average, and work hard to improve from average to good. But our push often seems to stop at *good*. Where sports are concerned, many good players become complacent, feeling satisfied that they have somehow "arrived" because they have a fat contract or score enough points to satisfy their ego. They're unwilling to commit to the pursuit of excellence, to take it to another level, trying to maximize the possibilities for themselves and their team. Some players do just enough to get by, just enough to fend off the teammate vying for their playing time, just enough to keep themselves on the court. They're satisfied with simply being "good enough." Players uninterested in excellence are content to be their team's leading scorer, think things are OK as long as they're getting the publicity they crave. They're unconcerned about trying to win championships, refuse to push themselves toward excellence. For them, being best on their team is good enough.

God gives each of us different gifts or abilities, and what works for one may not work for another. I understand that. But there's no reason *all of us* shouldn't want to excel, to recognize when greatness is possible and reach deep for it.

We've witnessed that push for personal excellence in sports, and it's something to behold. Players like Michael Jordan and Jerry Rice, for example, were blessed with great talent, but it was their *will* to be the best, their steadfast refusal to accept anything less than excellence, that took them over the top. Their desire to excel was second to none, and it showed. Just being "good" wasn't good enough for them, and they worked like crazy to achieve excellence. They squeezed every drop out of their potential by pushing for excellence. They demanded excellence from their teammates, too. They set a standard defined by it. Again, we all have different levels of ability, and some players will rise higher than others. That's the way it is. But while our talent levels may differ, each of us has a wonderful opportunity to squeeze the most from our effort and attitude, and it can take us farther than we ever imagined. Have you let simply being *good* become good enough for you? We must pursue our level of personal excellence. Otherwise, we're cheating ourselves and our teammates.

Commitment or Convenience

If we're committed to excellence, we must be able to remain focused when turbulence is swirling around us. Commitment is easy when the ball is bouncing our way, when our shots are falling and the score is in our favor. We're all committed then. But what happens when adversity arises, when our shots are off the mark or the coach is in our face or we don't get the grade we needed on that test or the big business deal we've been working on falls apart? How committed are we then?

We see it all the time in sports, players who seem strong and confident when things are going well but fall apart emotionally at the first sign of struggle. These players are quick to point fingers, to blame their teammates, to make excuses while hiding from commitment. They're in it only for themselves, and couldn't care less about true team success.

Our determination to stay committed during those tough times says everything about our character, about our potential for excellence. Do we succumb to setbacks and give up, or do we keep fighting and find a way to get it done? If we're used to being the go-to option on our team for scoring, for example and, all of a sudden, we're not getting the ball as much as usual for some reason, we can either complain about it, which causes division, or commit ourselves to helping the team in a different way in the meantime. If the situation calls for our teammate to shoot the ball instead of us, why not support the play the best we can by crashing the boards, by putting ourselves in position to rebound the ball and score if the shot is missed? Why not start learning how to *score without the ball*, as they say, instead of doing nothing if it's not in our hands?

At some point in our lives, we may be part of a team where racking up individual stats is more important to some of our teammates than winning games. And we may be absolutely powerless to control it. It's our responsibility to adjust to the situation, to try to become part of the solution instead of contributing further to the problem by indulging in self-pity. Because, no matter what, we can always control our attitude and effort.

Selective commitment, or commitment only when times are good for us, is called *selfishness*. That bandwagon is always full. Real commitment means staying true to purpose, to the best interests of our team, to continuing to fight for our teammates, no matter what the scoreboard says. Real commitment means adjusting our attitude and effort where necessary. It means doing whatever it takes to overcome obstacles on the path to becoming our best. It means persistence and perseverance, no matter how difficult our situation may seem.

Relationships without Achievement

Surrounding ourselves with the right teammates is a key to reaching our potential in life. Sharing our passion and purpose with others who feel the same way can lift the whole team to great heights. At the same time, however, nothing drags us down like teammates anchored in the past, stuck in fear and frustration and the muck of busted dreams.

These people thrive on *relationships without achievement*. It means their connection with us is covered in the dust of the past, is about what *used to be* instead of what's possible. They made token passes at their potential, perhaps, but fell short and chose to stay down. And they'd like to keep us down, too. They may be people we care about, people we once looked up to or with whom we used to have things in common. They may be our best buddies from the old neighborhood. But they may be affecting our ability to excel.

Productive relationships aren't anchored in the past, aren't slogging on that treadmill of tired old stories. They represent forward motion, and speak to possibilities and purpose. They're about shared commitment to becoming our best. It's great to reminisce with friends, to recall the old days, but we can't afford to get stuck in reverse. Relationships focused only on the rear-view mirror block movement toward improvement and can keep us from rising.

Relationships without achievement happen in sports, too. Players focused more on themselves than their team, for example, often flock together, and their collective egoistic approach can make things difficult for everyone around them. Players immersed in relationships without achievement care only about their individual stats, about the personal limelight. They aren't interested in true team success. When they're performing well, they make sure everyone knows. And when they're not, they try to drag others down. They're only happy when the focus is on them.

People who thrive on relationships without achievement aren't interested in possibilities. They're stuck in the same old places, running the same old schemes, with the same old toxic mindset, resisting our progress and refusing to hear of it. These people may still be dear to us, but we mustn't fool ourselves about what the relationship may be costing us. Remember, the best teammates are focused on forward movement.

AVOIDING THE BLAME GAME

Sound Bite Society

Ours has become a "sound bite society," with an endless loop of quick-serve quotes and clips firing across countless media outlets on numerous platforms. This is especially true of sports coverage, where snippets of game-winning glory are intertwined with images of angry-player outbursts in a whirlwind 24/7 news cycle. It's a blur of intense sound and symbolism, and the line between competitive and crazy has become muddied. There's a lot of *noise* out there, much of it mean-spirited, and it drives the ratings for all of these outlets. More than ever, we have to guard against letting those negative images penetrate our mindset and infect our game.

If we let it, the "Hype Machine" will suck us in and spit us out, leaving us to wonder what happened. Whether declaring this or that player or team the latest "greatest of all-time" or the worst that's ever been, listening to the hype mongers can distort our perspective. No matter what that Hype Machine claims, however, we must continue to focus on taking care of our business and becoming our best. Because that's all we can control. We can't control what the Hype Machine thinks or does or says about us, and it doesn't matter anyway. As long as we're working our hardest to raise our game and lift our teammates, on and off the court, we know what the real score is. If we fall into that trap of seeking approval instead of continuing to play with purpose, we're opening the door to defeat.

Buying the hype about how good we are is a ticket to disaster. No matter how many games we win or points we score or rebounds we grab, the only question that matters is, *are we making our teammates* better? Are we using our skills to support their skills to support the *team*? If it's only about us, about padding our stats or making the highlight reels to draw attention to ourselves, we're in trouble. The same Hype Machine that tells us how great we are today will write us off tomorrow, so buying in is pointless.

Doing our part to contribute to strong team chemistry means blocking out the hype, good or bad. It means taking a long look around that locker room and reconfirming what our real purpose means. It's a family affair, and we're in it together, no matter what. We can't let that "noise" outside our locker room creep in and affect our family circle.

That television reporter or newspaper writer doing a story about our team, for example, couldn't care less about how the story impacts our team chemistry. It's not their responsibility to make sure our team focus is where it needs to be. They're just doing their jobs, and that means selling their product. As a team, it's our duty to keep the hype and distraction outside our locker room. As a team, we know that hype and distraction is nothing but a negative for us. Opinion from anyone outside our locker room, outside our family, ultimately doesn't matter. It's not about what *they* say ... it's about what *we* do. If we start to buy what they're selling, for good or bad, we're in trouble.

I've always considered pep rallies during the season a hazardous part of the hype. Though the intention is good, to create buzz and energy and excitement for an upcoming game, players who aren't careful can get caught up in that hype and lose focus and the game before it even begins. Coaches must also be careful not to buy that hype. They must set the example of focus and keeping outside distractions from creeping into the team family circle they wish for their players to follow. Pep rallies are for celebration *after the job is done*, when the last game is won. Why celebrate when there's still work to do? The fans who are riding our bandwagon today will jump off tomorrow if we lose, so why invite it?

We must remain focused on controlling the only things we *can* control: our effort and our attitude. We must stay committed to bringing maximum effort and positive attitude each time we take the floor, blowing past the bandwagon jumpers and through the chaotic hype machine en route to making our teammates better. If we give in to the hype, we'll get caught up in ourselves and we'll begin to blame others when things fall apart.

Tearing down our teammates only costs us in the end. It destroys the team and blocks us from reaching our own potential. Blaming others causes conflict and indicates selfishness has overtaken our game. Our toughest opponent is ourselves, and the hardest player to defend is ego. If we let ego disrupt our game plan, we'll lose. No matter how much ego calls for the ball, we must stay strong and deny it.

Great players are selfless, always seeking to make those around them better. If we're focused on finding ways to help the team, the outcome will be favorable for all of us. If we keep our ego in check, we—and the team—will rise.

When the call doesn't go our way sometimes, when things aren't unfolding like we planned, we must accept accountability and avoid blaming others. Because when we point a finger of blame at someone else, *three fingers on that hand are pointing back at us*. It always comes back to us.

Mental Poverty

Blaming others for our troubles stems from what I call *Mental Poverty*, from a mindset that says it's always someone else's fault. *Mental Poverty* is a way of thinking that refuses ownership for the choices we've made and struggles they've caused. *Mental Poverty* means playing the role of victim. It complains about our circumstances instead of working to change them.

Kids mimic elsewhere the behavior they see at home, and if all they hear from parents is the voice of *Mental Poverty*, they'll begin to play that victim card, too. They hear that *Mental Poverty* voice so often that it becomes engrained in their thinking. It becomes part of them.

Coaches see it constantly with players. A player isn't receiving the playing time they feel they deserve, for example, and instead of looking in the mirror and holding themselves accountable for attitude and effort issues, they grasp for the easy excuse and blame the coach. "Coach doesn't want me on the team," they grumble. But if the coach truly didn't want the player on the team, they would have cut the player, not found a spot on the roster for them. If they're honest with themselves, players know full well why they're receiving playing time or not, and sharing the truth with their parents prevents confusion and frustration by parents.

Parents who wallow in a *Mental Poverty* mindset, however, are quick to fly off the emotional handle, convinced the coach is somehow keeping their child from success. These parents have tunnel vision when looking at their child's team; they're concerned only with their child's immediate gratification and couldn't care less about the team's bigger picture. These parents thrive on stirring up trouble with coaches or parents of other players on the team, claiming they're just looking out for their kid. Growing up, I'd have been aghast if my mom had interfered with our team family and confronted a coach about something like my playing time.

Parents who harass a coach or otherwise cause negative ripples around their child's team are robbing that child of a crucial opportunity for growth, cheating them out of a chance to learn and figure things out for themselves, to take an honest look inside and examine their effort and attitude and realize that complaining about their playing time doesn't solve anything. It's unacceptable for parents to confront a coach about how much playing time their child receives. Playing time should be merit-based and *non-negotiable* by a coach when dealing with players' parents. Parents who try to force their selfish agenda on a coach are setting an awful example for their kids, and obviously aren't concerned with what's best for the team. They couldn't care less about the team as a whole.

Unless a coach has crossed the sportsmanship line and is verbally or physically abusing players in some way, parents should remain on the periphery, offering support and encouragement to the coach and team and trusting that the coach is doing what's best for all. Because, frankly, aside from players' parents, nobody wants to see players succeed more than their coaches do! It's important that coaches not waver in the face of uncalled-for parental interference with the program, that they stay true to what they know in their hearts is best for the team. Coaches who cave to parental interference and attempt to change, who try to become something they're not because of meddling parents of players, are setting a losing tone and paving the way for premature exit. So long as coaches know in their hearts that they're doing the right things for the team as a whole, are helping players to grow and get better on and off the court, that their players are working hard and having fun, they must continue to trust themselves and stay true to their mission.

Parents with a *Mental Poverty* mindset pollute their child's approach to the game of life. They see things purely through subjective glasses, view them solely from the angle of their child's immediate success. They expect their child to be among a team's starting five, couldn't care less who the other four starters are, so long as their child is the fifth. To them, it's all about bragging rights, about an opportunity to puff out their chests with pride and ego to fellow parents. The selfishness inherent to a *Mental Poverty* mindset among parents doesn't just surface when challenges arise. It also emerges when kids achieve the solo success these parents covet. All teams, from pee-wee to professional, have a leading scorer, a player who averages more points per game than their teammates. This player is able to score points, of course, thanks largely to the efforts of their teammates, who pass the ball to this player or set picks for this player or rebound the ball or play great defense to put this player in position to score those points.

Parents infected with a *Mental Poverty* mindset seemingly stake their own, and their child's, worth to the points the kid scores in a game, convinced that the points a player scores is what matters most. These parents encourage ego at the expense of team triumph, and are happier seeing their kid win a scoring title or make an all-star team, for example, than seeing the whole team succeed. These parents typically couldn't care less whether or not their child is having fun playing the game, or even *wants* to play the game at all. To me, if a player isn't smiling much, they're probably not having fun with the game and may be feeling pressure from parents trying to "force" them to sports success, trying to be stars of the game through their children.

Parents with a *Mental Poverty* mindset see the game of basketball, or other sports, as a means to an *end* where their kids are concerned. They see it as an all-or-nothing proposition for their kids, where failure is not an option and their and their children's futures hinge on the kid's success in sports.

But sports should be seen as the means to a *beginning* for kids, not an end. The values kids learn by competing, by understanding how to become part of a team and contribute to something bigger than themselves, set them up for life success. The values kids learn by being part of a team are the same ones they'll need to become good spouses and parents and employees and members of the community.

Parents who plant that seed of sports as a means to an end with their kids are inviting destruction. Players who look at sports as a means to an end lose their identity when the game goes away, when they are no longer able to play for whatever reason. Players who see sports as a means to an end and do nothing but chase the money often end up broke, in more ways than one, their bank accounts busted and their self-worth in tatters because it was tied completely to a game they no longer play.

Players who use sports as a means to a beginning, however, focus on learning everything they can from the game, on learning how to be part of the whole, on being the best teammate they can be and doing the best job they can and letting the money chase them. And ultimately, it will find them.

Parents in a state of *Mental Poverty* can easily be identified at games. They are the ones constantly screaming at officials from the stands, convinced that every call that goes against their child's team is a bad one, and that officials must be conspiring to keep their child's team from winning. Once, while sitting in the stands watching a high school game, I saw the father of one of the players in the game get kicked out for berating and screaming profanity at the officials ... *and* at the coach of his son's team. To top it off, the player's father was a minister!

We all know officials make bad calls sometimes. But no player will ever play a perfect game, and no coach will ever coach one. We make mistakes. So why should we expect that officials will have a perfect game? They make mistakes, too. The most important thing isn't a bad call; it's how we *respond* to the call that matters. The moment we start grasping for excuses, like blaming officials for costing us the game, we're learning how to become *losers*. When we lose a game, if we're honest with ourselves from a player and team perspective, we can examine the results and find opportunities we didn't take advantage of, or mistakes we made that helped our opponent. We may claim we lost because of a bad call, but we know better. One call doesn't determine a game's outcome. Our own inability to make every possession in the game count is what puts us in a hole. What if we'd protected the paint better, or rebounded better, or hadn't turned the ball over and given our opponent additional opportunities? *That's* where the game was lost. On and off the court, each opportunity, each possession, is critical for us, and we must make the most of them. It's important that we maintain a *possession-by-possession mindset*, from tipoff to the final buzzer. We can't afford to let up or take possessions off. If we do, we're opening that door to possible defeat. If we stay focused on playing the game the right way, things will usually work out well for us in the end. We won't be left reaching for excuses, claiming a bad call cost us the game like people stuck in a *Mental Poverty* mindset do.

Reasonable Adult Voice

If we're honest with ourselves, we know why we come up short, and it isn't because others want us to fail. We're responsible for our lot in life, and if we don't like it, it's up to us to change it. It begins and ends with how we *think*, about ourselves and what is possible for us. That voice of truth inside us is what I call the *Reasonable Adult Voice*, and successful people are always tuned to it. The *Reasonable Adult Voice* cuts through the blame game, says we're responsible for improvement and there are no short cuts, that effort and attitude dictate our ability to overcome adversity and reach our potential. It says we must focus not on empty solo success but on the pursuit of lasting team glory.

The *Reasonable Adult Voice* asks what we can do to help our team succeed. It says it doesn't matter if we score two or twenty points, so long as the team wins. It says no matter the choices we've made in the past, we have the power to change our present. The *Reasonable Adult Voice* says self-pity and pointing fingers will keep us stuck on the bench, but holding ourselves accountable for our effort and attitude can take us places we never imagined.

The *Reasonable Adult Voice* says being part of a team is about something bigger than ourselves, that the team's success means more than our own stats. It says adversity reveals our true character, says it's easy to talk a good game when the ball is bouncing our way, but how we respond to adversity defines us. The *Reasonable Adult Voice* says our behavior must be congruent with our dreams, that only through sound decision-making can we make special things happen. The *Reasonable Adult Voice* says it's about finding answers, not making excuses. That doesn't mean it's easy. It's not supposed to be. But no one else can do the work for us. It's ours to handle. If we're serious about improving, we'll make the necessary sacrifice. The *Reasonable Adult Voice* is there to guide and encourage us. It's up to us to listen and act.

Apples and Trees

I believe the old adage about apples not falling far from their trees is true. Kids model the behavior they see from their parents, either positive or negative. If that behavior is guided by the *Reasonable Adult Voice*, it helps to build self-confidence and a strong foundation for success. If it's dictated by *Mental Poverty*, however, that misery and gloom will contaminate the child's mindset.

I'm convinced that, as coaches or teachers who encounter children dealing with *Mental Poverty* at home, it's our duty to pick up the apple and toss it as far from that poisoned tree as possible. Working with kids facing *Mental Poverty* at home is a delicate issue and must be handled with care. Often, these kids are filled with emotion they've been uncomfortable releasing at home.

They're seeking an opportunity to let it out, to vent their concerns to someone they trust.

In discussion with kids about what's happening at home, we must avoid expressing judgment about the parents. Respect for the parent-child relationship is essential. We must understand that, in most cases, if the parents *knew* better, they'd *do* better. That acknowledgement should be balanced by helping the kid realize that, no matter their parents' struggles with addiction or behavioral issues or anything else, those dark clouds needn't hang over their own futures, also.

One time, the father of a player on my team demanded to meet with me and our school principal, alleging I had verbally abused his son in practice. It wasn't true. The truth was, his son was struggling with attitude and effort issues and had become frustrated over a lack of playing time. Rather than sharing the real reason for that lack of playing time with his father, so that his father might understand, the youngster buckled to the prevailing *Mental Poverty* mindset he'd been exposed to at home, seeking someone else to blame and painting me as the bad guy.

During our meeting, the father became hostile and aggressive toward me, refused to hear reason, stepped verbally far over any line of decency or respect. He railed about my alleged "abuse" of his son, claimed I was out to get his son, and challenged me to prove otherwise. It was clear he was trying to get me fired, rather than trying to solve a problem involving his son. I looked his son in the eye and asked him to confirm whether the charges his father was making about me were true. He declared that they were. He and I knew better, of course, but the kid knew it was too late to backtrack, knew he had to stand behind his and his father's claims or endure hell when they got home if he admitted otherwise. If at all possible, it's important that a coach or teacher not create a wedge between child and parent, but I wasn't about to have my career jeopardized by outlandish allegations. They'd left me no choice. So I told the father that, indeed, I did care about his son, shared with him the story of how I'd held his son in my arms after practice one night as the distraught boy described the awful beating his father had given his mother that morning. And I mentioned how it seemed awful coincidental that the boy's mom, who never missed a game, happened to miss one the night after the apparent beating. The father grew quiet. His rage disappeared. He knew it was true. He gathered his son and left.

My players and students often share with me what's happening in their home, what's going on with their families. They need an outlet for their emotion or anxiety. They trust me, and I value that trust. I had been there for that player in perhaps his darkest moment, yet, because of the *Mental Poverty* mindset that dominated his home life, he'd succumbed to blame-seeking and excuse-making. His father's behavior in that meeting was out of line and I was forced to let him know I knew the truth. I cared about his son on a far deeper level than something trivial like playing time.

As coaches or teachers or mentors, it's our duty to be there for kids, to counsel them, to listen, to try to help them through the tough times, to support their dreams and develop good character, no matter the difficulties they may be dealing with at home. It's important to let them know that, while they love their parents, they don't have to travel the same destructive path of abuse or addiction or blame tossing. They have an opportunity to break that cycle. In my case, I explain to kids that I've been there, that I know what they're going through, that my father abandoned me when I was young and I could've continued that cycle with my sons. But I was determined to break that pattern instead, and was committed to being a good father to them. When kids realize you've been there and dealt with similar circumstances, they find it easier to let their guard down a bit and begin to trust.

PLANTING SEEDS

Coaching the Whole Kid

Coaches employ numerous methods to motivate players, but I believe verbal or physical abuse is absolutely unacceptable. Where verbal abuse is concerned, I believe negative words destroy kids. I know from experience that player and coach relationships aren't rosy all the time; far from it. Players who aren't performing to their potential should expect to hear about it from their coaches. And players who desire to reach their level of personal excellence should thrive on that feedback. Coaches are obligated to try to get the most out of their players, to do their best to help young people develop.

There's a fine line for coaches, however, between challenging a player to reach for their best and verbally attacking the player. While each player reacts to a coach's motivational tactics in their own way, few respond well to being constantly berated. Any temporary spike in a player's performance seemingly resulting from a coach's verbal abuse will quickly fall off and will pale versus the short and long term emotional damage to the kid.

A coach's words are crucial seeds to a young player's emotional growth. If the verbal seeds planted by a coach are abusive and character-damning, an emotionally-damaged player will likely develop. Conversely, coaches who plant positive verbal seeds aid players in reaching their physical and emotional best. Coaches must always be mindful when tending that "verbal garden" of player development. The seeds planted by a coach, positive or negative, determine the type of fruit that grows from them. It goes hand in hand.

I'm convinced it's much more effective for a coach to take a positive verbal approach in working with players. That doesn't mean sugarcoating or ignoring areas where obvious improvement is needed. If a player repeats mistakes, for example, it's the coach's duty to determine why and to try to correct it. But along with holding the player accountable for improvement, coaches must be willing to hold *themselves* accountable, also, to figure out why they fell short in connecting the dots of understanding for the player. The coach must then adjust their approach to the player accordingly. Addressing areas where improvement by a player is needed should never deteriorate into a verbal attack on the player.

I learned early in my coaching career about the fine line between challenging kids to be their best and verbally attacking them. I believe coaches' verbal attacks usually stem from ego, from being more concerned with their own success than with development, especially emotionally, of their players. As a young coach, I mistakenly believed my self-worth was determined by my record (i.e. wins and losses). I didn't understand that coaching was my *job*, but my won/lost record didn't define me as a *person*. Early on, my coaching approach was all about *me*, not about the kids. I was constantly in players' faces during practices and games, for example, telling them everything they would *never be* instead of encouraging them about what they *could become*. My approach was rooted in discouragement. I tried to control everything and didn't give the players a chance to grow emotionally.

During a game one night, an official said something that stunned me. "Satch," he told me, "you need to relax! You're always pacing the sideline, uptight, screaming at your players. You're too involved. You have good players. You should trust 'em, and let 'em play."

The official was someone I knew and respected, but his comment seemed out of line to me. *How dare him*, I thought. I told him to mind his own business and focus on his officiating. But I couldn't stop thinking about what he'd said. During a timeout, I was angry with our players for some mistakes they'd made. "Come on, fellas!" I barked. "You've gotta learn to *think* out there!" At that moment, I caught a glimpse of myself on a courtside camera. I didn't like what I saw. I was ranting to the players about not using their heads on the court, but it dawned on me that I had never given them a chance to do it. I had tried to control every facet of the game. Anytime we got the ball, for example, our players instantly looked to me for a play call. It was the same way on defense. No matter the situation, they were apprehensive, worried about what I was doing on the sidelines. I had become a distraction to them. I had kept such tight control that I hadn't allowed the players to figure things out for themselves, to trust their own knowledge about what was happening in the game and adjust accordingly.

Though his comment offended me at first, it didn't take me long to become thankful for what that official said to me because it made me a different coach, a better one, and for the right reasons. I began to sit more during games, wasn't standing or frantically pacing at courtside all the time. I realized I'd been caught up in ego, seeking to validate myself as a young coach at the emotional expense of my players. That realization reached to the core of why I'd become a coach in the first place, which was to help mold and impact young lives in a positive fashion, on and off the court, to prepare kids for the bigger challenges of the game of life.

Unfortunately, I made a coaching misstep later in my career that was embarrassing and hurtful to me and, much more importantly, to one of my players. During crunch time of one of our big games at Northland, the player made a crucial turnover. In the locker room after the game, I berated him in front of our team, telling him all the things I believed he wasn't, instead of supporting and encouraging him and telling him all the good things he represented. It was bad enough that I said those things in the first place, but inexcusable that I'd said them in front of the team. He was angry and embarrassed. My poor behavior weighed heavily on my mind that night, and I couldn't sleep. The next morning, I called the player to my office. I told him that error he'd made in the game didn't compare with the mistake I'd made in berating him. I explained that, instead of handling the situation responsibly as an adult and coach, I had failed him. I had let him down and I was terribly sorry. He'd made that error while playing hard to win, while giving his full effort, and that's all a coach can ask.

I knew the player would never forget what I'd done, but I asked him for forgiveness and told him it would never happen again, to him or any other player. To his credit, he forgave me. I called the player's parents, too, to explain what I'd done and tell them how sorry I was for having let my emotions get the best of me and taking it out on their son. I was wrong, and I had to admit it and learn from it. It never happened again. Thankfully, my relationship with the player grew stronger.

I realized that our words to kids either *build* or *destroy*; there is no middle ground. I realized that, in a larger sense, no matter how badly a player might be struggling, I should be grateful if they kept showing up, kept pushing to get better in practice and during games, because it meant they cared. I began to make sure players knew how much I appreciated their effort, how thankful I was that *they kept showing up.* I was committed to doing everything I could to help them improve, on the court and off. As a teacher, I've always taken that approach in the classroom, too. No matter how poorly a student may be doing in my class, no matter how much they may be struggling, as long as they keep showing up, it's my responsibility to do whatever I can to help them get better. On the court or in the classroom, I believe if a kid is showing up but not improving, then it's my fault. *I* have failed *them*, not the other way around. I've fallen short on their behalf. It's my obligation to help them succeed.

I adjusted my verbal approach to players when addressing them, as a group and one-on-one. I made it a point to begin my talks with them on a positive note, by pointing out something they were doing well. Then, we'd talk about areas where they needed to improve. At the end of our discussion, I'd reinforce another positive point with them. I believe it is important to finish our talks with players with encouragement.

I learned that no matter how frustrated a coach may grow with parts of a player's game, the coach must guard against letting that frustration become a blanket indictment of the player. So long as the player's effort is strong and attitude is right, so long as that "want to" is there, the possibility to realize potential remains.

The power of our words is immense. Once spoken, a coach's or teacher's or parent's words cannot be taken back. Kids may forgive a coach or parent for antagonism, but they don't forget. If a coach's approach is rooted in constant hostility, the coach is in it only to feed their ego. Some coaches believe they can force improvement by bullying a player, but they're wrong. All they do is lose the player emotionally for good, because that player tunes out. There's no room in the game for coaches who continually bully, who make a habit of tearing players down. Constructive criticism or occasional animated instruction or discussion in the spirit of competition is one thing, but relentless antagonism by a coach purely for ego's sake is another. Coaches who are in constant *"attack, attack, attack!"* verbal mode with their players may survive for a while, may win some games, but *the game itself* will ultimately identify and root them out. Their antagonistic ways eventually catch up with them. They keep pushing players toward a dangerous edge, and it ends for these coaches in ugly fashion.

Coaches who cross the line with constant verbal abuse are caught up in ego and have lost their sense of purpose. When they lose that sense of purpose, they lose their professionalism, too, and the door leading to possible physical abuse of players is wide-open.

Where physical abuse of players by a coach is concerned, it is egregious and unacceptable. There's no place for it in the game, ever. Any coach who steps over the line physically with kids, who loses control in a fit of rage and puts their hands on a player with ill intent, is adrift in ego and concerned only about themselves. They're in the game for all the wrong reasons. Aside from their obvious disregard for a player's physical and emotional well-being, a coach involved in physical abuse of players is exhibiting incredible *selfishness*. Because crossing that line means a coach has inexplicably attached their entire sense of *self-worth* to their players, means a coach believes his personal value is determined exclusively by what his players do on the court.

Coaches who verbally or physically abuse their players suck that all-important *sense of purpose*, the will to win the *right way*, by trusting each other and helping our teammates become better, from those players. Coaches should be caretakers and nurturers of that sense of purpose, not *crushers* of it. Coaches who abuse are often enabled along the way by goal-oriented school athletic directors caught up in their own ego, who put winning above all else and turn a blind eye until things explode.

In an odd way, from a selfishness perspective, there's little difference between an abusive coach and a player who disregards their teammates in an effort to "get theirs," whether it's scoring points or pursuing other personal statistics, outside the best interests of the team. Though one may be more repulsive on the surface, both ultimately stem from selfishness, from a toxic mindset that says "I'm gonna verbally or physically abuse these *players*, or coach this *game,* or try to score *these points*, for ME!'" To these coaches or players, the team's best interest doesn't apply.

In both cases, any consideration by that coach or player of the importance of *team*, of the value of *we instead of me* thinking, is buried in a search for solo glory. And that's selfishness.

From a spirit of sports perspective, I liken such selfishness to a kind of "competitive crime" of varying levels. I believe that coaches who verbally or physically abuse their players, for example, are committing the worst level of crime, the first degree; they're obliterating their players' sense of purpose, blowing away an opportunity to lead by example, to teach players how to become part of something bigger than themselves, to help them understand that winning *the right way* will always matter most. For a coach, that's the ultimate crime.

Players who are focused solely on themselves, on "getting theirs" at the expense of others, no matter what, are committing second-degree competitive crime. Their selfishness will kill the team, especially in crunch time. It will destroy team unity and poison team purpose. The decisions and actions of these players are all about what's best for *them*, and they don't care who knows it.

Players guilty of third-degree competitive crime are the sneaky ones, the ones who *pretend* to be purposeful, who *act* like the team is most important, players who say the right things and play the right way ... for a while. These are the players who let up in intensity when their team is ahead in the game, who start jacking up shots or slacking on defense or taking possessions off, thinking no one will notice because their team has the lead. They're the ones who show that they *understand* what playing with purpose means, but who choose to play with purpose only when it's *convenient* for them. Their selective commitment wrecks a team's purposeful flow.

Like I said, some players respond to a coach's motivational methods differently than others. It's critical for coaches to take the time necessary to *get to know their players* and to avoid assumptions about them. Verbal or physical abuse by a coach is an obvious sign that the coach has no interest in getting to know players, isn't concerned with learning about what makes players tick as *people*. For a coach, getting to know a player means looking beyond their physical skills, their athletic ability, and seeking to understand their mental and emotional makeup, too. It's about making a commitment to players as *people*, not just athletes.

As coaches, we ask and expect players to improve, but we have an obligation to them to keep getting better *ourselves*, too. We have to try to be better each day than we were the day before. We must constantly evaluate and adjust our approach to players, our communication with them. We must always attempt to teach and challenge them in a positive way, and avoid attacking them or tearing them down. Coaches who build with positive words establish a foundation of trust with their players, and trust is essential to sustained success.

Coaches who care only about the "player" part of a kid, the athlete part, are in it for themselves, willing to win at all costs, and see nothing wrong with abusing players. These coaches shouldn't be surprised, then, when the team implodes during crunch time, when trust by players in their coach makes all the difference between championship banners and defeatist dissension. Success during crunch time may be influenced somewhat by a coach's X's and O's, but is largely dependent on the level of trust that exists between players and coach. Trust comes from *love*, and love isn't possible if a coach hasn't made the effort to get to know players mentally and emotionally. If trust between coach and players exists, players' confidence during crunch time will be evident and the results will show it.

Aside from a kid's physical skills, coaches must focus on developing those mental and emotional pieces, too. If a coach fails to develop those parts, fails to help kids understand the long-term value of playing with purpose (i.e., *for others*) on and off the court instead of pursuing temporary, ego-based goals, those players will never reach their potential. The coach may help maximize the kid's *physical* skills, but what about the rest? Added together, those developed thirds, the physical, mental and emotional, equals *One*, the complete person. The total player. Developing each of these thirds, and not just the athletic part, should be the mission of all coaches. Coaches may help players become better *on* the court, but must never lose sight of the more important job of helping them to improve *off* the court.

It's the same way in the classroom. As a teacher, it's important for me to take a vested interest in my students, far beyond the next test or homework assignment. It's crucial for me to take the time to talk with them, to *share with them*, to get to know how they think, what makes them tick, mentally and emotionally … to see them as more than just bodies in chairs in my classroom for an hour a day. Rather than taking the easy way out and teaching the *subject*, it's my duty to teach the *kids*, and the only way to do it is by connecting with them, by trying to get to know them as *people*.

It's important they see me as more than just a teacher, too. I want them to know I care about them, that they can trust me, because once trust exists, we can begin to break down barriers. I must be open with them, be willing to share my values or vulnerabilities. As in any relationship, the more we trust each other, the more progress we can make together, the further toward our potential we can push.

Trust is a Two-Way Street

The ability to establish trust between a player and coach is a two-way street. While coaches must be held accountable for their protocol in dealing with players and should strive to develop the whole young person, not just the "player" part. Players, in turn, must be held accountable for the effort and attitude they bring to the task. They must constantly evaluate their level of commitment, and be truthful with themselves about their desire to keep improving. If they're content with being *pretty good*, for example, where the possibility of excellence exists, if they're concerned with pacing themselves to get through practice instead of giving it their all each time out, if they're asking everything from the coach but giving less than their best in return, the relationship won't work.

As a coach, I always had a lesson plan for our players, like I did for students in my classroom. The lesson plan for the team consisted of all the fundamental ground I wanted to cover in practice, all the objectives I hoped we could accomplish during our allotted time together each day. While I hoped we could fully cover the targeted fundamental ground in each practice session, I understood it wouldn't always happen. That understanding was tethered to the effort level of our players.

If we had covered most of a particular day's lesson plan, for example, and I saw that our players were dragging, were spent from having already given every ounce of energy in their tanks to that point in practice, I stopped pushing and put the lesson plan away and we were done with practice in a positive way. While there was still ground we hadn't covered, there was no point in trying to push the kids for more when I knew they had nothing left. My recognition that our team *as a whole* had given everything they had each day wasn't clouded by any single player's inability to keep up with the group. An out of shape player who consistently lagged behind the others in drills because of reluctance to push himself was welcome to get all the rest he needed ... on the sidelines. There was no need to yell at or try to embarrass the player for slacking. There was no need to say anything at all to the player. Standing sheepishly on the sideline while watching his teammates go through drills and continue to grind it out delivered the message.

Coaches who drive players relentlessly in practice, who continue to push players beyond what they have to give with little concern for the team dynamic, are opening the door for trust issues and complacency to creep in. By disregarding the boundaries of reasonable player expectation, coaches inevitably force players into survival mode; player focus moves from *thriving* in practice to just trying to *get through it*. That attempt to survive is where complacency begins.

As players realize that a coach doesn't care, refuses to let up and will keep pounding them mercilessly for more each day no matter how hard they work, they start to pace themselves in a negative way just to survive practice. It's no longer about getting better, but trying to endure. Coaches in tune with their team, who know when players have given their all and are willing to acknowledge it and ease up a bit, even in subtle ways, gain the trust of their players. Those players understand it's about giving their all from the first drill of practice, and that once they've left it all out there, it's done and the coach has their backs.

Positive Team Chemistry Doesn't Just 'Happen'

Chemistry is a popular word in sports, especially where talk about successful teams is concerned. "That team has great *chemistry*," we say with reverence, as if some magical blanket has appeared from nowhere and mysteriously enveloped a team. We typically think of *chemistry* in sports from a positive perspective. But chemistry has a flip side, too. It can be negative. In fact, if ego and selfishness creep into a team's mix, it can be downright toxic.

Good chemistry among teammates doesn't just *happen*. Coaches are responsible for first establishing a *culture* around a program that enables good chemistry to brew. That culture should be "family-based," where each player knows the coach and their teammates have their backs, are truly looking out for them and want what's best for them. It's a culture that says *we're all in this together*, no matter what happens. When a family atmosphere exists for a team, players feel love for each other and their coaches. When love exists, players can begin to trust, in their coach and one another and their own purpose within the team structure. When *trust* is present, players will give everything they have in the name of team purpose, without insistence on egoistic fulfillment. That's when special things begin to happen for a team.

For coaches, establishing a team culture conducive to good chemistry begins by making clear at the outset to players exactly what the program *stands for*, its ideals (i.e., integrity, work ethic, winning the right way, etc.), and insisting on accountability by all players to those core values. It continues with acknowledgment by the group that those core values cannot be compromised by players or coaches without consequence. It's essential that coaches help their players understand the importance of holding themselves and each other accountable to family (team) standards, and help them realize the significance of playing with *purpose*, for *each other,* setting aside focus on individual goals or glory in the name of ultimate team success.

Early on, it's critical that coaches identify and *define to players their roles* within the team structure so that players understand where they fit and what is expected of them. That way, coach and players are on the same page and there is little margin for misunderstanding. Jump shooters are expected to shoot jump shots, for example; post players are expected to handle their business in the paint and on the boards; slashers are expected to slash to the bucket; and *all* are expected to play tough defense. Each player knows his role. This eliminates confusion. When crunch time comes, when a game's outcome hangs in the balance, players know which teammate will be handling the ball, know which teammate will be taking the key shot. Bad players fight their roles, good players accept their roles and great players *dominate* their roles.

No matter how talented a player may be, they must be able to put aside ego and embrace their assigned role in the best interests of the team. They must be able to step outside of their own immediate wants and see the bigger team picture. Otherwise, synergy (good chemistry) among teammates cannot occur. A notable example of positive role-acceptance in the name of team purpose from my own experiences comes to mind.

When Trey Burke, the consensus national college basketball player of the year who led Michigan to within a whisker of the national championship in 2012-13, arrived as a freshman in our program at Northland High School in Columbus, he was chomping at the bit to start at point guard, and rightfully so. Trey was already well on his way to becoming a special player at the time, had been a standout for years as a youngster. But our point guard, senior Devon Moore, who went on to play at James Madison University and set the school record for assists there, had started for three seasons. Devon had worked his tail off for our program, had become an All-District player and an inspirational leader for us. He had earned his way and then some.

Though Trey believed he was more than capable of taking over point guard duties for us as a freshman (and he was right), he refused to let his ego get in the way of what he knew was best for the team at the time. Rather than complaining about his situation and causing division among his teammates, he accepted and embraced his role as Devon's backup that season, decided it was a valuable opportunity to make himself better by learning from a guy who had been there. Trey understood that his time would come, and when he took over as our point guard the following season, he was a better player for it. Trey has always been grateful to Devon for what Devon taught him about leadership and toughness and sacrifice.

Once player roles have been defined, and expectations for those roles are understood, team leadership will begin to emerge.

A leader, or leaders, of the team will step up and make themselves known. That assumption of leadership is a natural byproduct of defined roles for players. It can't be forced. None of us can force others to follow us. We can only work to put ourselves in position for them to want us to lead.

When team leaders step forward, they'll help set a purposeful tone for the club. They'll hold themselves and their teammates accountable. Effective team leaders will set the work ethic standard for the team, and others will fall in line accordingly. On our state championship team at Northland High in 2009, my son Jared and Trey were tremendous leaders for us. They led the way with their work ethic. They refused to be outworked. And they expected their teammates to give everything they had. When a team's best players are also its hardest workers, that team has an opportunity to be really good, and it proved true for us that season.

A coach's failure to establish an airtight, family-based team culture, or to effectively define player roles, opens the door to all sorts of problems for a team. It allows splintering of essential group unity to occur, allows for distrust among teammates, allows ego and selfishness to creep in, allows players to develop that poisonous "me" mindset that will eat away at the team and ultimately destroy it.

Leading by Example

Being an effective coach means helping kids understand how their decisions, on and off the court, impact *others*, including teammates and family members. Coaches who default to an indifferent, easy-way-out, "Shut up and play!" approach to their players are doing those players a huge disservice. Demanding that players do things a certain way, without helping them first understand why doing things that way may benefit them and their teammates, misses the larger coaching mark.

A coach must be willing to *lead by example*. It's the same with parents or teachers. We should never ask kids to do anything we're not first willing to do ourselves. We can't insist kids do things a particular way, without explanation, and then do it differently ourselves and expect kids not to question our leadership. It doesn't work that way. Leading by example means following the same rules as coaches or parents or teachers that we expect our players or children to follow. We must set the example of desired behavior for them.

I see the leadership double standard in action all the time at school. The drop-off zone for students in front of Northland High is designed as one-way in and out, to ease traffic flow at the beginning and end of the school day. All drivers, including teachers, are expected to enter the lot in the designated fashion. Doing so means it takes teachers a moment or two longer in the morning to reach our parking area, but the rules are in place for all to follow, teachers included.

Too often, however, I've seen teachers enter the parking lot the wrong way on purpose, forcing their way through the lot just to save a minute. Their actions show that these teachers think they're above the rules. And the students notice it. They realize that the same teachers who preach to them about following the rules ignore those rules themselves. It sends a conflicting message to kids, says those teachers aren't being "real" with them.

If, as coaches or parents or teachers, we set an example of skirting the rules, why should we be surprised when our kids do the same? Like it or not, kids follow our lead. We're all parts of the whole, all members of the same team, and we must all pull in the same direction to accomplish special things. We can't pick and choose which rules we follow in life based on what's convenient for us and expect our kids to do otherwise. We must set the example we want them to follow.

Sometimes, we set a bad example for kids by telling them what they *want* to hear instead of what they *need* to hear, by letting them do what they *want* to do, instead of what they *need* to do, in situations where key emotional growth is possible for them. We short-circuit their opportunity to learn valuable life lessons by kowtowing to them, by letting them get away with things they shouldn't because we're seeking to gain approval from them. It's a recipe for disaster.

A friend and fellow high school coach once shared his frustration with me over the embarrassing way the assistant principal at his high school dealt with players on the school's highly-successful basketball team. Apparently, this assistant principal had two sets of rules where students at the school were concerned—one set for players on the basketball team and another set for the rest of the students.

This coach told me that the assistant principal went out of his way to accommodate players on the basketball team, including allowing them to skirt rules all students were expected to follow, to ensure that the players were happy and the team might continue to win. He said the assistant principal allowed the players to hang out in the hallways for extended periods of time during the school day, doing whatever they wanted to do, while all other students were expected to be in class.

According to the coach, the assistant principal even brought lunches to the players and allowed them to eat in the lobby of the school, where students were typically not permitted to be while classes were in session.

When he heard about what was happening, the coach reported it to the school principal, who confronted the assistant principal and remedied the situation. The assistant principal had set an awful example for the players, had become an enabler to their poor judgment because winning games was apparently more important to him than showing kids the importance of accountability.

Leading by example means pushing aside our personal agendas and staying committed to keeping kids on the right decision-making path in life, no matter whether they're star players or anyone else. Hearing and seeing the truth from us today, whether they want to or not, will be of benefit to kids tomorrow.

In trying to address the difficult issue of drugs in high school sports, there has been increasing talk by administrators about the idea of random testing for players. While I believe there is no place for drugs in sports at any level and appreciate the general intention behind the idea, I believe it's an important opportunity for school administrators, coaches, athletic directors and anyone else associated with high school sports programs to step up, to show kids the way by *example* and submit to drug testing *themselves*, too. Why take the easy way out and lay the burden solely on the kids? If it's important enough that we're asking *them* to do it, why shouldn't *we* be willing to do it, also? That's what leading by example means.

As a coach, I always made it a point to attend study table with my players. Study table is a designated time for a team to meet and work on class assignments, homework, etc. It is a time of group accountability. Some coaches don't bother to attend study table with their players. That's fine. But I felt if study table were important enough that I expected my players to attend, I should be there with them. I'd work on lesson plans for my sociology class during study table, or read a book. But the key is that I was there with my team, pulling in the same direction to get things done. I tried to model the behavior I hoped they'd follow.

For coaches or parents or teachers, simply *talking* it to kids isn't enough. We have to *walk* it, too. Like the old saying goes, our actions speak so loudly others can't hear what we say. We can talk all we want, but it's our actions that show what we're really about.

I believe leading by example comes down to the difference between *subjective* values and *objective* values, and our subscription to either. Subscribing to *subjective values*, for example, means we'll do the right things only because we're "forced" to do them, because someone is watching us or paying attention and we may be exposed if we do otherwise. Subscribing to *objective values*, on the other hand, means we consistently do the right things because we know they're best for *everyone*, even when we know we can get away with doing what benefits *us* the most. If we're subscribed to *subjective* values, are doing the wrong things just because no one is around to see us, we're asking for trouble. Our bad karma will come back to bite us when the game is on the line. Because *we play the game the way we live our lives,* our habit of bad decision-making will ultimately be exposed when crunch time comes and our true character is revealed.

Subscription to *objective* values isn't a sometimes thing. Doing the right things for the right reasons consistently means commitment. It means not taking plays off. Subscription to objective values is what effective leadership is all about.

We can't demand that kids follow our lead. It doesn't work. Rather, we must put ourselves in position for them to *want* us to lead. That happens when they trust us, and we can only build that trust by the example we set for them, by modeling the positive behavior we want to see from them. If it's good enough for them, it's good enough for us.

Goals mean 'Us,' Purpose means 'Others'

Following rules and setting a good example for others is part of *living with purpose*, which means staying true to what's best for the team, no matter what others may try to make us believe. Living with purpose means commitment to using our skills to support *those of our teammates*, to helping them improve, to making a positive difference in the lives of others without any *What's in it for me?* motivation.

Living with purpose is the *opposite* of striving to reach goals. Striving to reach goals typically signifies self-centered thinking, focuses more on what's best for *us* individually than on what's best for the *team*. In other words, goals are mostly about serving *ourselves*, but purpose is about serving *others*. Goal-centered thinking is about trying to prove *ourselves*, but a purpose-based mindset means trying to *improve* the lives of others.

The only way our striving to reach goals can impact others in a positive fashion is if those goals are a natural byproduct of *team purpose*, of a mission to *win for each other*, not in a hidden search for solo glory. So long as our focus is we-centered, our effort based on making our teammates better, on supporting the skills that support ours (synergy), the team has a chance to be successful. The moment we step off the team purpose page, however, in an effort to be the leading scorer or make flashy plays while ignoring the fundamentals to draw attention to ourselves, we're engaging in the selfishness inherent to goal-based thinking. If we're focused only on finding individual success and unconcerned with helping our teammates get better, we're missing the mark.

We all want to win as many games as possible, of course, and our ultimate mission as members of the team or parts of the whole should be excellence, or championships. In team sports, individual excellence means understanding the group's larger objective, understanding our roles within that structure, and working our hardest to fill them. It means asking ourselves what the group needs most from us to succeed, and doing it—with no excuses or complaints. It means we're determined to get that rebound no matter what, because it's important to *the team*. It's not about our individual stats. It's about giving our all for our teammates, without seeking anything from them in return. Playing with purpose means we're doing the right work, for the right reasons, and trusting the process. Because *living with purpose, playing with purpose*, is contagious, and if we're doing it, sooner or later our teammates will do it, too. And when a team is playing with purpose, special things happen.

Ultimately, our mission as pieces of the whole should be about giving *purposeful effort*, about trying to reach our level of personal excellence in synergy with, and in support of, the team. If our motivation is simply to achieve self-focused goals, our impact on others will be minimal and fleeting at best. If we're coming from a place of purpose, however, our actions will create a lasting positive legacy. We'll have helped to improve the lives of others in a way that endures, even after we're gone.

Increasingly, it seems our society is about immediate fulfillment, about doing whatever we wish now and worrying about the consequences later. That approach is toxic to our team and our own potential. We see it constantly in sports, especially during crunch time: the player who abandons purposeful team approach and launches an ill-advised shot in search of solo glory. That wrong intention costs the player plenty, but it costs the team much more. The motive is selfish. The action arises from ego. Selfish thinking is a losing proposition. If our hearts are in the right place and we're focused on helping our teammates get better, our game will prosper. It's a simple but powerful equation: *heart right + mind right = game right.* If our hearts are unselfish, our mind will follow and our game will rise. Then, we win *and* the team wins. That's what playing with purpose means. It means playing the game for the *right reasons.* If our thoughts are selfish, if we're focused only on our own stats or success, it doesn't matter how talented we may be; we'll come up short when it matters most. It's easy to gain attention in a negative way, to stand out by acting out or tearing our teammates down. That's a loser's game plan. If we're playing with purpose, defending our values and rebounding from adversity with tenacity, staying above the fray in a positive way, we're bound to win. We mustn't waste time worrying about the haters out there. We can't control what others say or do, and we'll never please everybody, anyway. But we can *always* control our effort and our attitude.

As long as we stay committed to our teammates and we keep improving, it doesn't matter *what* our opponent tries … they won't be able to stop us. *That's* living with purpose. Because, in sports and life, the real competition is *inside us*, anyway! That's where the game is ultimately won. As loud as those pessimistic voices on the periphery may seem sometimes, if we're living with purpose, they'll drown in defeat.

Winning Isn't Always Defined by the Scoreboard

Winning, on and off the court, isn't always reflected by the final score. Make no mistake, the final score matters, of course, and if we're gonna play the game, we should play to win. Otherwise, why bother? If we're not playing to win, we're doing a disservice to the game, our teammates and ourselves.

But sometimes the scoreboard can be deceiving. Just because a team wins, for example, doesn't automatically mean its players are committed to each other. Likewise, just because a team loses doesn't mean its players have their own agendas. That winning team might soon be exposed, with a selfish player or two about to show their true colors when crunch time comes and the spotlight shines brightest. And that losing team might be in the process of developing an atmosphere of "family," of accountability to each other that bodes well for eventual success. Nobody goes undefeated in life. We all face obstacles, and sometimes we come up short. Sometimes our opponent is just better than we are.

While no one likes to lose, I believe there is value in defeat when it happens. There are lessons in losing that, if we're paying attention, will make us stronger and, hopefully, better. As painful as it may be sometimes, we can't let the bitterness of defeat get the best of us and squander our opportunity to learn. And sometimes, that learning happens the hard way. It's up to us to pull the positives from those seemingly negative experiences. When we lose, the only way to improve is by taking those positives tucked into our defeats and building on them. Right or wrong, it seems players often practice harder after a loss than they do following a win. Perhaps it's just human nature.

As much as we hope to avoid it, sometimes winning lulls us into a false sense of security, makes us believe we're better than we are, makes us think we can get away with giving less than our best and that things will still turn out OK for us. Unfortunately, it sometimes takes a loss to open a team's collective eyes and gain its fullest focus. We should be open to examining our losses and an honest evaluation of our performance, to studying what we tried to do and why it didn't work, to seeing how doing things differently the next time may yield the desired results for us.

When we lose, we must ask ourselves if our opponent is truly better than us. *If we played that team ten times*, in other words, *would we win or lose most of them?* If we honestly believe we'd win most of them, if we truly feel we're the better team, then we must take a hard look at our effort and attitude to make sure it backs up that belief. Because it doesn't matter how talented we are; if we're not giving our best attitude and effort each time out, we're opening the door to defeat. We must be able to accept and adjust where necessary, to avoid complacency, to avoid the trap of doing the same old things, the same old way, even when the situation screams for change.

Win or lose, what's most important is making sure we're working hard to *improve* each day, to be better individually and as a team today than we were yesterday. No matter what the scoreboard says, we must continue to strive for personal and team excellence. If we're consistently giving our best and looking for ways to help our teammates improve, the scoreboard will be in our favor most of the time. We'll win all the games we're supposed to, will be fortunate to win some that we probably should have lost, and, when we lose, it'll be because our opponent was simply better. It won't be because we weren't prepared or got outhustled or were selfish.

It's the same way in life. If we're waking up every day committed to purposeful living, to making the right plays for the right reasons, we'll come out on top most of the time. And even when we lose, we can hold our heads high because we'll know we brought our best.

WINNING THE RIGHT WAY

Only Cheating Ourselves

At its core, what makes winning special is that we know the possibility of *losing* always exists, no matter our opponent. It doesn't mean we dwell on the idea of defeat, of course, or that we don't believe we'll win. Confidence is essential to success. And preparation feeds confidence. If we've worked hard and prepared as necessary, our confidence will shine through when the game is on the line. No matter how good our team or how much an underdog our opponent, however, we can never take victory for granted. Winning is never guaranteed. That's why we play the games … because you never know.

But what if we *did* know? What if cheating gave us an upper hand, so the results were less in doubt? How would we feel about our victories then? Cheaters disregard the sweat and blood and sacrifice that makes winning the right way special. They ignore integrity and scoff at sincerity in a search for shortcut glory. To them, commitment and character sit the bench while selfishness plays the star.

A coach or program that cheats cannot eliminate all possibility of losing, of course, but is willing to roll the dirtiest dice to minimize it. Cheaters lucky enough to win a championship will always bear the burden of knowing that banner hanging in their gym represents deception. There can be no pride associated with it.

Cheating to win costs a coach or a program plenty, but it costs the players more. As a coach, nothing is more important than helping kids understand the power of purpose, of contributing to something bigger than themselves, of using their skills to support their teammates and serve others.

Cheating is the ultimate selfishness, stemming from an empty pursuit of money or self-worth. The decision to cheat is driven by one or the other. Coaches who cheat desperately crave the spotlight. It's all about ego. They'll do whatever it takes, in the worst ways, to win so they can keep moving up the coaches' ladder (i.e., land bigger and better jobs), and kids are the casualty. A friend of mine once put it like this: Kids will meet our expectations for them, no matter how high or low those expectations. And cheating is as low as those expectations get.

Coaches who cheat during the recruiting process, who are willing to cross clear morals and values lines in win-at-all-costs desperation to land players they covet, will never gain the respect of those players they get, no matter how many games the team may win. They'll never get the best out of those players. Because no matter how supportive the players may seem publicly about the coach, they know in their hearts what the coach is really about; they know how far over the line the coach went to get them to commit to his program. Deep down, they know the coach doesn't care about them as people and cares only about hijacking their skills to further the coach's selfish pursuits. The players will never respect that coach.

Coaches who pressure teachers to change a player's grade just to keep that player eligible are failing the kid where it matters most. These coaches are in it for the wrong reasons, happy to trade a kid's chance to learn important life lessons for a possible cheapened championship. On the surface, it may seem to the player that the coach is looking out for them by trying to keep them eligible to play, but the coach is actually making it obvious that winning is more important than the kid's future. And the players unwittingly defer. And their teammates defer. And others in the program turn their heads in silent approval. Once coaches open that door of dishonesty, anything goes and there's no turning back. There are too many tracks to cover. The team may win, but at what cost to the players? When coaches cheat, it's the kids they cheat most.

Schools that hire coaches who cheat ultimately get what they deserve, including the shame of being forced to remove those tainted championship banners from the gym rafters and names from the record books. Inexplicably to me, however, the cheating scandal buck always seems to stop at coaches and occasionally at athletic directors, who rightfully pay for their wrong decisions with their jobs and reputations. But what about the presidents of these universities? Why should they get a pass? They aren't above the fray of unsavory goings-on in their athletic programs and should be held accountable for the ensuing mess, too.

No matter their attempted public relations spin or after-the-fact denials, these university presidents can't expect us to believe they are completely unaware of what's happening in their athletic house before it finally catches fire. In fact, I believe the win-at-all-costs way of doing business for which coaches are rightfully condemned is sometimes encouraged, perhaps even initiated, by university higher-ups hell-bent on the pursuit of victory and the acclaim (see: *money*) it brings for their institutions.

I believe that, in some cases, coaches who may be straddling the values fence anyway are nudged to the wrong side by impatient school administrators uninterested in growing a program the right way and intent on a quick dirty fix. These administrators are willing to forsake the futures of kids in the program in their desperate attempt to "win now." Coaches who are paying attention to the signals these administrators give during the job interview process should have a solid feel for what the administration they're about to get involved with stands for, so claiming to be victims of that unsavory administrative approach after the damage is done is unacceptable.

It works both ways, of course. The coach/administrative relationship is a two-way street, and reciprocal respect and accountability is essential for the partnership to work. On the flipside, I'm convinced that if a school or university has done its proper homework in hiring a coach, they're aware of potential trouble with that coach. Because typically, coaches who cheat have somehow shown a pattern of it, operating in the shadows of untruth until the full extent of their rule-breaking is exposed. When the manure hits the fan and the school is under public fire, these coaches slink away to other programs with administrations desperate enough to win that they'll discount the coaches' misdeeds ... for a while.

These coaches aren't interested in doing things the right way; they'd rather get better at being wrong. They scheme and keep moving, always trying to dodge the bullet they themselves fired, until they finally exhaust their options and have nowhere left to go but out of the game. And once gone, these coaches have zero endorsement value to corporations and brands because the stain of cheating stays with them. Their dishonest ways are a flashing red light to anyone who cares about good character. These coaches are unwanted as spokespersons for coaching organizations and unable to go out on their own terms. They live with the weight of knowing they disrespected the game and destroyed opportunities to impact others in a positive way.

The wreckage they leave behind is enormous. Schools that hire suspect coaches deserve the public relations damage and financial fallout that inevitably come from it. Unfortunately, the players and others in the program who have done things the right way are impacted unfairly by the blows of scandal.

The win-at-any-cost way has claimed countless promising futures, all for an egoistic grab at illusory acclaim. Schools (see: presidents, athletic directors, boards of trustees) that hire shady coaches who happen to have a strong win/loss record are just chasing the money, desperate for a shot at a championship and willing to sell their integrity to get it. They make their own miserable bed and deserve to lie in it. But the players and fans and other supporters of the program who are doing things the right way don't.

Playing with Purpose

It may seem odd, but I believe winning the right way is *easy* to do, not difficult. It simplifies our mission and cuts through the noise and ego. When we're *playing with purpose*, for that name on the *front* of our jerseys instead of the one on the back, our decisions are largely made for us. And those decisions will lead us down a positive path. Winning the right way happens before we ever step on the court.

It means *playing the game the way we live our lives.* If we're being good teammates, holding ourselves accountable at home and work and school, handling our obligations, respecting ourselves and others, it will show during crunch time on the court. And if we're not holding ourselves accountable, that'll show, too. It's called karma. We can't ignore our obligations and expect that carrying that baggage won't weigh us down in crunch time.

Winning the right way means seeking selfless success. It's realizing the game of life isn't about the *me*, it's about the *we*, about using our skills to support the whole. It means playing with purpose. When we're geared toward team, we'll blow past ego and ill advice on the way to collective glory.

The power of playing with purpose is what makes sports special. It defines championship teams. We've all seen teams loaded with talent that come up short up short in the biggest games due to lack of purpose. The team may be filled with great athletes, but if those players are playing only for their egos, the team will fall short.

Championship teams consist of players focused on what's best for the whole, who believe in *One Heartbeat* and have bought in for their teammates, who will gladly trade personal stats to be part of something bigger. They're playing for the name on the front of their jerseys and everything it represents, not the name on the back. That's playing with purpose.

Respect the Game (Life)

No matter how successful we may be in life, one thing is for certain: If we're disrespecting others, looking down on them because they're different from us or dismissing them because they don't meet our vision of what they should be, we're tempting karma in a negative way. And when we do that, we'll lose.

Respect is fundamental to maximizing our potential. Respect for ourselves and our teammates and those with whom we share purpose, of course, but also for our opponents and others who might not do things exactly like we do. It's important for us to try to understand where others are coming from, because this isn't a one-size-fits-all world. If we're closed-minded and unwilling to consider other perspectives, we'll miss valuable opportunities to learn and improve and help our teammates get better.

If we believe the game of life is only about us, if we're prone to egocentric displays and playing for *ours* at the expense of *others*, if we're always taking and never giving, we'll eventually find ourselves and our dreams alone on the bench.

My Grandpa Jim always said that a person wrapped up in themselves makes a very small package. Egoism is an empty pursuit. We see it all the time in sports, that "disease of me," as the great coach and leader Pat Riley dubbed it in his terrific book, *The Winner Within*. Players absorbed in themselves, their careers littered with selfish choices, with no thought about consequence, with lots of excuses and no commitment to change, wrongly assuming that talent trumps character.

It's the same on or off the court. We may slide by on talent alone for a while, but if we aren't respecting the game, karma will step in and settle the score. Because *talent can take us places poor character can't sustain.* No matter how high we rise because of our talent, if our character is poor, we'll eventually crash and burn.

Respect is essential, and if we're playing without it, the game will find a way to frustrate us. No matter how talented we may be, the game was here long before us, and will be here long after we're gone. So we'd better respect it. That means looking for ways to get better, to help our teammates improve, to use our skills to support our teammates, which feeds the success of the whole.

Respecting others doesn't mean blindly buying in to whatever they're doing and abandoning our sense of values. If they're running a scheme or treating others poorly, living recklessly or looking for shortcuts, they're obviously out for themselves and don't deserve our respect. But if they're working hard each day, treating the game with respect and trying to contribute in a positive way, they're helping to strengthen the team, even if their approach may be different than ours.

The ability to respect others starts with respecting ourselves, with doing the right things for the right reasons and trusting in God's plan for us. We'll never please everybody, and we'll screw up sometimes, but if our intentions are pure, our good karma will help us get back on track quickly.

Unfortunately, there's a tendency in our society today to tear others down in an effort to build ourselves up. Too often, we take shots at people who are working to try to make a positive difference in the world, smiling to ourselves when they stumble and offering insincere applause when they succeed. People too scared to follow their dreams and make a positive impact themselves usually resort to criticizing others who are actually doing it. Instead of wasting our precious time and energy slamming others for their efforts, however, why not give them the respect they deserve, take a hard look at ourselves and try to change for the better?

Improving ourselves is the first step to helping our teammates get better, which is the first step in establishing essential team synergy.

Synergy means each player, each *part of the unit*, feeds the next part, which feeds the whole. It means all parts combined are stronger than any individual piece. I believe strongly that, for any team or organization, championship-level success is impossible without synergy. To me, each letter of the word represents an essential piece of the success puzzle:

S= Selflessness. Selflessness means committing ourselves to doing everything we can to help make our teammates better, *without expectation of, or focus on, individual glory.* Pat Riley once described selflessness as "giving without asking for anything in return, trusting that everything due us will arrive in the jet streams of our hard work." In other words, we don't have to push it, don't have to force it. If we're doing the work, it will come to us. If we're committed to helping our teammates improve and succeed, are doing the right things with the right intentions on their behalf and for the good of the team, our good karma will come back to us. That's selflessness. Selflessness is trusting without fear, committing ourselves to helping our teammates succeed without knowing the outcome but giving our all anyway. Selflessness is trusting that commitment to our teammates' success will eventually put us in position to succeed, also.

Y = Yeoman's work. At Oberlin College, our mascot was a Yeoman. There are a few dictionary definitions for the word, each essentially referring to *servant* or *service*, to doing the best job we can on behalf of others. Here's the definition I like best: *service performed in a loyal, useful or workmanlike manner … especially in situations that involve a great deal of effort.* On the road to success, there's no substitute for hard work. There's no shortcut. If becoming successful were easy, everyone would do it, right? It takes constant effort and perseverance, requires giving our best no matter how difficult the circumstances. All that hard work is what makes reaching success so sweet. In sports, success is often defined by winning championships. That's what true competitors strive for, of course. But success also means working to maximize our personal excellence. Sometimes, the scoreboard can be misleading. I've had teams win games that, though the victories looked good from the outside, I knew were merely fool's gold because we weren't doing what was necessary to get better, weren't truly committed to each other, to selflessness. On the other hand, in some games we lost, I felt good about our team because I knew we were improving, that our work ethic and commitment to purpose were there. On the road to success, we have to do the work.

N = Never Quit. Michael Jordan once said that he could accept failure sometimes, but could never accept the idea of quitting. Quitting, to me, is about lack of heart. It's about giving up instead of working to maximize our personal excellence. It's about looking for shortcuts and taking the easy way out, which leads only to negative places. Quitting means cheating our teammates and, worst of all, cheating ourselves. We all come up short sometimes in life; we all face adversity at some point. How we respond to that adversity defines who we are. Anyone can talk the talk when things are going well for us, say the right things when the ball is bouncing our way. That's easy. But it's what's in our *hearts* that matters most and speaks the loudest. And our actions reflect what's in our hearts. Quitting says we're weak at heart, that we don't believe we're worthy of success and aren't willing to do the work it takes to get there. All of us taste defeat at some point, but the only time we fail is when we quit. When we lose, the naysayers will be quick to write us off, to pat us on the back and tell us good luck next time and assume they've seen the last of us. But we have to keep coming, keep bouncing back. That's what champions do. They might lose, but they never quit. They refuse to give the naysayers the satisfaction of seeing them give up. They take the valuable lessons from their losses and use them to get better, come back stronger, help their teammates improve.

E = Every Possession. It's important for us to make the most of each opportunity in life, to bring our best to each situation, no matter the circumstance. Whether we're ahead by twenty points or behind by twenty, we can't afford to take a play or a possession off because we never know which possession may be the one that turns the tide or takes us to the next level. Taking a possession off means we've begun playing the scoreboard instead of the game and opens the door to defeat. We can't take possessions for granted. I've always believed that we play the game the way we live our lives. What happens during crunch time for us on the court is a direct reflection of how we're handling our business off the court. To me, the two can't be separated. It's a karma thing. If we have to be told to take the trash out at home, for example, odds are that someone will have to tell us to rotate to the baseline on the court, too. Why force others to ask us, when we already know what we're supposed to do? If we're taking possessions off away from the court, not being the best family member or employee or student or citizen we can be consistently, not respecting others or offering a hand where it's needed, we're throwing away valuable possessions, and it will come back to bite us. It will cost us during crunch time. It will keep us from greatness. Making the most of every possession means knowing what we need to do for the team and doing it, without procrastination, without our teammates having to ask us. Putting things off means we're missing an opportunity to get better, to create good karma for ourselves. Make every possession count because they all make a difference!

R = Relentlessness. Relentlessness means no matter how tired we may be, or how much our opponent has worn us down, we'll never show it. We'll never quit. We'll dig deep and keep fighting. Relentlessness means no matter how long or far our opponent runs from us, we'll keep coming. It means no matter how long *they* chase *us*, they'll never catch us. We'll always outlast them. It's a warrior mentality that says, *"One of us will eventually drop, and it's not gonna be me."* Because the first player or team to let thoughts of giving up creep into their psyche will lose. Relentlessness is the melding of our mental and physical tenacity. It's finding a zone beyond that first wave of fatigue. I used to tell my players that getting into shape doesn't mean running until you're tired; it starts with the work you do *after* you're tired. There's a second wind inside all of us. Many people never tap it, however, because they stop when they lose their first one. Relentlessness is our determination to thrive, mentally and physically, in that place where tired begins.

G = Giving with Purpose. Giving with Purpose means using our skills in the name of helping our teammates to improve, knowing that their improvement feeds the good of the whole, which in turn cycles back around to help us succeed, too. It means seeking collective glory instead of the individual spotlight, trusting that our efforts are contributing to something bigger than ourselves. Giving with Purpose is the opposite of selfishness, goes beyond our individual stat sheet. It seems many players today are so focused on getting theirs that they lose sight of the concept of *team* altogether, sacrificing potential group greatness in search of hollow solo acclaim. The karma deck is stacked against selfish players. A few may stumble into good fortune, but most will never win a championship. They may get close enough to sniff it, but they'll ultimately fall short. Why? Because championship teams face adversity along the path, and it takes every member of the team pulling in one direction to emerge unscathed. It takes a *One Heartbeat*, "We're all in this together!" approach. Selfish players, however, splinter that approach. They shrink from adversity because it forces them to look in the mirror, to hold themselves accountable. Giving with Purpose means giving up our good shot so a teammate can take a *better* one, means helping our teammates on defense instead of being the defender who has to be bailed out all the time. We all need help sometimes, but if we're never giving it and always seeking it, there's a problem. Giving with Purpose is about steadiness and consistency, not flash or hype. Giving with Purpose equals *reasons for winning, not excuses for losing*.

Y = Yielding Nothing. *Yielding Nothing* means "no mercy" on our opponents, finishing the job with a flourish instead of coasting to the finish line, no matter how far ahead of the other team we may be. It means commitment instead of contentment. *Yielding Nothing* means we embrace the pressure that comes with being the hunted, the biggest game of the season for teams trying to dash our championship dreams, and refuse to fall back to that pack. *Yielding Nothing* means we understand there can be little margin for error in our performance if we expect to stay on top. It speaks to our burning desire to keep improving, to always focus on playing the game instead of the scoreboard. *Yielding Nothing* means keeping our guard up and keeping selfishness and complacency from creeping in, means keeping the door closed on our opponents. *Yielding Nothing* means if we're behind, we'll keep fighting, knowing it's in those moments of adversity that our true character is revealed and real growth possible.

Winners think 'We,' not 'Me'

Players and coaches who understand it's not about them individually, but about their role in helping to create synergy for the team, will enjoy the best the game has to offer. Those who fail to understand it are asking for frustration. And sooner or later, they'll find it. No player can succeed without help from teammates. A star player may make a great shot, for example, but they can't do it without help. What about the teammate who set a screen for the star player to free them for that shot, or who made a great pass to the star player, or who rebounded or stole the ball to give the team possession in the first place? It takes a whole team.

Much of the important work players do during a game to help their team win will never be seen in media highlights. For the media, it's all about driving ratings or selling copy, and soaring dunks and three-point bombs sell. That's the way it is. But those players in the spotlight should always be quick to credit their teammates for that unglamorous but essential work, like the teammate who hedged well on screens and prevented penetration in the lane, for example, or who banged the boards at both ends to prevent second-shot opportunities for the opponent, creating them for their own team instead, or who put the clamps on an opposing player defensively. The highlight shows will always feature points and flash, but those other pieces are perhaps more important. Great players recognize that, and are quick to make others aware of it, too.

Great players rarely use the word *I* when talking about their team, especially when the team is winning. Instead, they say *we*, while distributing appropriate credit to their teammates and coaches. To great players, it's all about a team atmosphere of *family,* of togetherness. Great players only say *I* when accepting responsibility as a leader for their or their team's poor performance. They'll say "*I* need to do a better job of this or that," or "*I* just didn't make the play when we needed it," etc. Great players shy from saying *I* when the team is winning, and accept ownership when it isn't. They're about *purpose*, and they respect the game.

It's the same with great coaches. No matter how successful they've been or how many championships they've won, great coaches rarely say *I* when talking about their success. They're quick to say *we* instead, to point out how the team is playing *as one*. They credit their players for making them look good. They never verbally pat themselves on the back. Conversely, when their team is struggling, great coaches hold themselves accountable first, as in, "*I* could have done a better job of preparing our team to play" or "*I* didn't make the adjustments we needed," etc.

The *pronouns* coaches use when referring to their team, especially when the team is struggling, say it all. And their players hear those pronouns loud and clear, for good or bad. Coaches who default to using divisive words like *they*, for example, when discussing their struggling team are asking for trouble. Coaches who use the word *they* when talking about their team during tough times send a message of division between them and their players, a message of accountability avoidance, of trying to separate themselves from the team's struggles.

No matter how poorly a team may be playing, coaches should resist referring to their players as *they*. It should always be about *we*, about togetherness, about how the team refuses to give up, about a team's "singular heartbeat." After all, teams are simply reflections of their coaches. Coaches who *coach* for the wrong reasons often recruit players who *play* for the wrong reasons, too, and it inevitably shows in the product on the court. If coaches are trying to win games simply to validate themselves, to show people "how good" they are, it will be reflected in the self-serving attitudes of their players. Players are extensions of their coaches.

Great coaches respect the game and their players at all times, especially in public. And that respect is defined by *we*, not *me*.

Fundamentals, not Flash

Nowadays, it seems there are more players at all levels, from professional to Pee Wee, getting caught up in "flash," in trying to make a highlight-reel play instead of executing effectively with sound *fundamentals*, often to the detriment of their teams. With the glut of sports talk shows that exists across all media platforms comes an endless loop of highlights, most of which consist of outrageous dunks or three-point shots or players charging down the court thumping their chests or thrusting their fists in egoistic fashion after making plays that, quite frankly, they are *expected* to make anyway.

There's nothing wrong with players displaying positive emotion and competitive fire, urging their teammates on, exhorting each other to raise their collective game. It's great to see preparation and confidence in action, see players who have worked hard to put themselves and their team in position to rise to the occasion and dominate the opponent. But that individual confidence should always be used as fuel for the greater group purpose and never degenerate into a "Look at *Me!*" mindset or behavior. That's selfishness. The name of the game is getting better, of course, individually and as a group, and when a player or team has prepared effectively to win, that confidence will shine through when it matters most. The spirit of competition says we should not only want to win, but to crush our opponent, if possible. Stepping off the established team page of purposefulness in an attempt to draw individual acclaim, however, is destructive. Seeking to impress others with flash, needlessly trying to turn a simple play into a spectacular one just to make the highlight reel, speaks to ego, to trying to stand out from our teammates in a negative way. Great plays are part of the game, of course, but the best ones happen *naturally* as a part of team purpose and without the forced flash of selfishness.

Executing consistently with sound fundamentals instead of trying to impress others with "Look at *Me!*" flash puts us in the best position for sustained success, on and off the court. Fundamentals may not make the highlight shows but they're the essential building blocks to championship performance. Fundamentals will never let us down. They can always be relied upon. They represent *purpose in action*. They represent doing the right things for the right reasons with no shortcuts to selfishness. They represent practice and preparation. Ignoring the fundamentals will prevent us, and the team, from reaching our potential. Because *we play the game the way we live our lives.* The way we're living will be reflected in our performance during crunch time on the court. The two can't be separated. If we're executing sound fundamentals, like working hard in school and at our jobs, like obeying the law, like treating ourselves and others with respect, like looking to give instead of trying to take, our execution will carry over to the court, also. We'll be prepared to embrace our roles, be purposeful teammates and play the game the right way. At the same time, if we're ignoring our school work, if we're showing up late to our jobs, if we're getting into trouble or causing problems for others, if we're disregarding *the fundamentals of life*, we'll fail to execute effectively on the court, too. We'll be lousy teammates, reckless and selfish, concerned only with getting ours at the expense of others. And that's fundamentally wrong.

Three Stages of Becoming a Champion

A coach's responsibility to the team begins with helping players *learn how to compete*, which is the first step to becoming a champion.

Learning how to compete sounds simple, perhaps, but without a strong grasp of that essential building block, winning consistently and capturing championships can never happen. *Learning how to compete* is the gateway through which good things develop, for player and team. *Learning how to compete* begins and ends with effort, with commitment to playing our hardest, individually and collectively, on each possession, no matter our opponent. *Learning how to compete* is not about trying to be perfect; it recognizes that we'll make our share of mistakes along the way. It asks, however, that those mistakes occur only while we're giving our best effort. *Learning how to compete* means realizing there are individual consequences when we don't play our hardest (i.e., a seat on the bench). If we're not playing our hardest, we're failing to make the most of the gifts God gives us and we're blocking our potential success. We're hurting our teammates, too. *Learning how to compete* is about establishing a unified team work ethic and an understanding by each player that anything less than best effort is unacceptable. *Learning how to compete* means that, though we may still be losing more games than we'd like, our effort in those losses can no longer be questioned.

The second step to becoming a champion is *learning how to win*. This means we've established the foundation of consistent best effort and have built on it by minimizing our mistakes, especially during crunch time of games, when the outcome hangs in the balance. *Learning how to win* means there is no longer room for the errors we accepted while learning to compete.

Learning how to win means making the most of each possession, on offense and defense. It means we're playing with a collective confidence borne of trust in our teammates, knowing we're all on the same page and playing with the best interests of the team in mind, playing with *synergy*. *Learning how to win* means ego has been replaced by acceptance of our individual roles within the team framework. It means we're executing our game plan to the best of our ability, and have begun to turn the competitive corner.

Learning how to win means that, as a team, we're no longer beating ourselves, are no longer failing to protect the paint or giving up cheap baskets, especially when the game is on the line. It means we're passing up our good shot so our teammate can take a better one. It means we're consistently doing what's necessary to be "in the game" at the end, to be right there in crunch time with a great chance to win it. *Learning how to win* means we've begun to come out on top in some of those tight ballgames, too.

Learning how to play like a champion is the final piece in the puzzle of individual and team excellence. It becomes possible only after we've learned how to win consistently, including the lion's share of those close contests. *Learning how to play like a champion* means we're constantly hungry, have become consistently purposeful, that we're playing for the name on the front of our jerseys instead of the one on the back. It means we're climbing the championship mountain and we won't let anything stop us.

Learning how to play like a champion means we *expect* to win every game we play, no matter our opponent, and anything less is unacceptable. It means we've become the prohibitive favorite, have moved from the hunter to the hunted, and are prepared to take our opponent's best shot each time out. *Learning how to become a champion* means relentless focus and execution, no matter how far we're ahead or determined our opponent may be. It means "going for the jugular," delivering the knockout punch at our first opportunity instead of letting the other team hang around and gain confidence. *Learning how to become a champion* means continuing to handle our business away from the court, knowing that our behavior "out there," consistently making the right decisions for the right reasons, creates our karma as a player. After all, we play the game the way we live our lives. The two can't be separated. *Learning how to become a champion* means staying humble, no matter how many games we've won. It means realizing the game is much bigger than any of us individually, that it was here long before we arrived and will be here long after we're gone. So we'd better respect it.

Don't Pull Up Short on Your Potential

As players or coaches in the biggest game there is, we all know that at some point, the buzzer will sound and the game will be over. No matter how talented we may be, none of us can avoid that final buzzer. Sooner or later, in sports and life, our last chance to take the floor will be gone. While none of us has the final say about when the game ends, we're obligated until then to make each possession count. That means maximizing our effort and attitude and minimizing our mistakes to give our team the best chance to succeed. Because when the *team* wins, we *all* win, and that's what playing the game should be about for us. That's playing with purpose.

Winners understand it takes maximum effort from the opening tip to that final buzzer to succeed, and they don't take plays off. They know that making unforced errors (bad decisions) or attempting to pad their stats instead of helping their teammates signifies selfishness, and invites trouble for themselves and the team. They realize it takes only one player stepping off the team page to destroy everything the team has worked for.

When that final buzzer sounds, we should be at peace, knowing we played the game the right way and gave it everything we had, that we left it all on the court and our teammates were better because of it. We should be satisfied, knowing we didn't cheat the game or ourselves.

If our attitude is poor, if our work ethic is weak, if we're in it just for us, we're betraying the game, our teammates and ourselves. We may have all the talent in the world, but if we're not utilizing those six inches between our ears to maximum capability, we're pulling up short on our potential. And that's a sad legacy to leave.

Education is the Key

In sports, we know winning begins with mastering the fundamentals. No matter our talent level, if we fail to grasp the fundamentals, we'll never reach our potential. It's the same in life. God gives each of us our gifts, our ways of impacting others in positive fashion. But we can only fully develop those gifts by understanding where they fit and how best to use them. And that means mastering the most important fundamental of all ... education.

Education is about what we feed ourselves mentally each day, and that "mental food" is our choice, no matter where we are in life. Education defines us. Education, or lack of it, separates us from the pack in a good or bad way. It's the key that unlocks our potential. It helps us understand the playing field, how to get in where we fit in and create the impact on others we desire.

Education starts with reading. Reading allows us to understand. It's the foundation from which good things spring. It's the vital first link. So why don't we read more? As a sociology teacher, I ask my students this question all the time. If we know reading unlocks possibilities for us, why don't we make the time to do it? What are we choosing to do instead?

There's an old joke in the African-American community that is painful to hear. Unfortunately, the truth often hurts. Here's the joke: In the African-American community, if you want to hide something valuable, just hide it in a book and it'll be safe, because no black person will ever look there. While drastic, perhaps, the joke's inference is telling: Books in our urban communities are mostly ignored, especially by youngsters. But the more we read, the better we're able to organize our thoughts. The better we're able to organize our thoughts, the better we'll be able to write. It starts with reading.

As a coach and teacher, education has always been the priority for me. A crucial part of education is helping kids to identify all the tricks they unwittingly place in their own paths that keep them from realizing their potential. The choice kids make to *not read* tops that list of tricks.

Reading helps to expand our minds, informs our thinking, enables us to see beyond our own little world and consider other ideas and beliefs. Reading makes it possible for us to step outside our experiences and see things from someone else's perspective. It helps us to envision the bigger picture in life. Reading inspires us to use our imagination and can be a terrific source of entertainment. It improves our vocabulary and helps us learn to write better, too.

Unfortunately, however, many kids mistakenly equate reading with boredom. Instead of thinking and using their imaginations and learning to discover for themselves by reading, they'd rather someone just spell things out for them, give them some conveniently summarized nutshell of the way things are. It's *easier* for them that way. They don't have to think. It's easier to just be told or to watch television. Much of the content our kids consume nowadays holds little or no real educational value, and plenty of it is filled with negative images and messages. These negative messages creep into kids' mindsets and plant themselves there. They work to keep kids from becoming their best.

Another trick I see kids falling for is obsession with their electronic "toys," including the cell phones with the latest and greatest capabilities. Don't get me wrong, I'm all for technology because, ultimately, it exists to help make our lives better. I have a cell phone, too, like everybody else. But increasingly, it seems many kids now depend on those phones to entertain them 24/7. Unfortunately, that "entertainment" often rears its head in the classroom. It's an avoidable distraction that costs kids plenty. The price they're paying is thinking and learning how to develop their minds. They may believe they're getting away with something by fiddling with their phones in class, but the joke is ultimately on them. It's a distraction from progress. It's a trick they don't have to fall for.

Education helps kids understand and attempt to eliminate one of the dirtiest tricks in our society today, which is the ignorance of intolerance. The destruction caused in our society by discrimination is immense and unacceptable. Why should someone else's race or religion or social status or sexuality become a fire pit of hatred for us? We're all part of the same team, all God's children. What right does any of us have to judge another? We must accept our teammates for who they are, not condemn them because they're different from us. We should encourage them to shine. What matters for each of us is that we're working hard each day, respecting others and the law and contributing to society in a positive way. If we're doing that, we'll have no time for hatred.

On and off the court, it's impossible for us to perform at our best if we're not in harmony with the game (life), if we're disrespecting the game or stirring up trouble for our teammates. Bullying or antagonism of our teammates is a cruel and dirty trick that costs kids plenty, and there is no place for it in our schools or anywhere else. Winners always treat others with respect. They understand that, just because someone may not possess the skills we possess, for example, or looks different from us or comes from a background that's different from ours or doesn't wear the same type of clothes we wear, doesn't mean we're not all equal as God's Children. We all have our unique gifts to offer. None of us is better than anyone else, and if we think we are, we're headed for trouble.

School can be a brutal place for kids somehow perceived as different, kids who, for whatever absurd reasons typically decided by a "cool" few, fail to earn a stamp of acceptance as equals. As I mentioned earlier, I was much bigger physically than my classmates as a teenager. Because of my size, I was considered different than the other kids in a negative way, and I became a target of their ridicule. They taunted me, called me names.

When I'd show up at other kids' houses to hang out, their parents looked at me like I didn't belong. It caused me a lot of emotional turmoil and took a physical and emotional toll on me.

I recall a classmate of mine in high school named Terry Darce. Terry was a great student, got fantastic grades, paid attention to the teachers in class, never got into trouble. He consistently pushed himself harder in his studies than everyone else. He loved school, loved to learn. Unfortunately, other kids ridiculed him for it. They thought he was different, considered him a nerd. They called him derogatory names, made it difficult for him whenever possible, let him know loudly and clearly that they felt he didn't fit in.

I had learned from my own experiences with bullying as an early teenager the pain it can cause, and I refused to go along with the crowd and participate in it where Terry Darce was concerned. Instead of giving him a hard time like the others, I talked with Terry, expressed my admiration for his academic ability. I showed him the respect he deserved as a student, and, most importantly, as a human being. It's important that we stand strong and not buckle to peer pressure in life, especially where disrespecting others is concerned. We must stay true to ourselves and our values, no matter what the crowd may say about us.

Later, when I returned to Columbus from Oberlin College on summer break, I needed a job. I applied for a warehouse position with a plastics company. The man who hired me? Terry Darce, that so-called high school bookworm and misfit, who had gone on to excel in college and had become the company's personnel director.

Even when others try to tell us we don't fit in, claim we're too much of this or not enough of that and say we'll never measure up, it's important for us to stay true to ourselves, to learn to embrace the way God made us and keep pushing. I stuck out in a unique way as a teenager because of my size, and it was tough at first. But when I finally learned to accept it as a positive, my outlook changed. The size that made me an outcast early on proved to be an asset later, became an advantage to me as an athlete. It helped me to become a better basketball player in high school and get an opportunity to play in college, where I could gain an education. Getting that education is what inspired me to want to work with kids, which ultimately led to coaching and teaching. It all came full circle, back to the size that had caused me such trepidation as a youngster.

Ultimately, it comes down to this: *What kind of impact do we want to make on others in life?* Do we want to impact them in a negative way, disrespecting them and causing problems for them because they're different from us, like bullies do? Or do we want to take the high road, impact them in a positive way, encourage and inspire them like real teammates do? There is no in-between; we're either helping others to get better or we're getting in the way, and that gets us nowhere. If we're embracing the gifts God gives us and using them to support our teammates, we'll all win together.

Whether coaching or in the classroom over the years, my mission has remained the same: to help kids realize their self-worth, their true value, to understand all that is possible for them if they'll commit to bettering themselves and avoid the tricks that hold them back. On the basketball court, just like in life, we can succeed only through commitment to getting better each day and trying to help our teammates improve. That means making the most of the gifts God gives us, doing the best we can and trusting that good things will come to us in the process.

The commitment to purpose that is necessary for kids to succeed on the court or in the classroom is the same commitment required for them to become good fathers or mothers or husbands or wives or employees—good teammates—later on. It's crucial for us to help kids realize they have the power to choose their path in life, and that path, either positive or negative, is established by their early acceptance or rejection of accountability, of commitment to doing the work to put themselves in position for eventual success. If they're willing to commit *now*, their road will be smoother later. If they're not, they'll have a bumpy ride. Rather than scrambling after the fact to escape trouble, or picking up the pieces after a self-made storm fueled by lack of focus, kids can make it easier on themselves down the road by doing what's necessary now. If we're fooling around in the classroom, not taking our studies seriously, if we're ignoring our responsibilities at home or work, we're not wasting time ... we're wasting *ourselves* instead. Because we don't own time! We don't own those minutes that tick away. The sun will rise and set each day no matter what. But we *do* own our effort and our attitude, and if we're just going through the motions and not giving our best and letting those minutes tick by, we're only wasting ourselves.

Lack of commitment by kids to education, to doing the work required to get better and put themselves in position to succeed, means they'll likely continue the sad cycles of transience and broken relationships and poverty so prevalent in our urban communities. Unfortunately, too many of our kids are grappling with negative circumstances at home, forced to cope with parental abuse or absenteeism or addiction issues or other chaos. It's our duty to help kids understand that, no matter how bad things may seem for them sometimes, they own the power to break that cycle of negativity and build the path for a bright future.

Where education is concerned, our kids aren't the only ones guilty of falling for the tricks that block their paths to progress. As teachers and administrators, we must avoid the dangerous mistake of getting caught up in ego, in the delusion that our students are there to serve us. It's the other way around. Our job is to serve *them*. If we get caught up in authority, in believing that being in charge is what matters, we're cheating them.

As educators in this country, we're guilty of some of the worst tricks of all where our kids are concerned. Instead of testing to what kids know, for example, to what they have learned, our educational system is geared toward testing what they *don't* know.

And too often, kids don't know it because we aren't teaching them effectively! We're so focused on teaching to the test nowadays that we're ignoring our kids' needs in the process.

The huge holes in our approach to education in America are apparent early on in the process, when we begin moving kids through the system and on to the next grade level simply because they've passed just enough classes, regardless of obvious red flag areas of failure. For example, a kid struggling with mathematics might flunk math classes for several years in school, yet continue to be bumped up to the next grade level because they've passed just enough classes in other subjects. How can a teacher possibly make up in one school year for that child the ground that's been lost during the previous several? And on and on the cycle goes.

How can we expect our kids to take academics seriously when we continue to pass them through the system regardless of repeated failure? Why should we expect them to take state testing seriously when they know we've continued to blindly move them through the system? Isn't our job as educators to help make kids better? Too often, we're conditioning them by our actions to take on a *Mental Poverty* mindset, to believe they're going to pass even if they fail. And that faulty thinking follows them after high school, when reality hits for them and things fall apart and there's nobody there to help pick up the pieces.

Kids don't care how much we know until they know how much we care, and if we're focused only on ourselves, wrongly convinced that *they* need *us* more than we need them, we're blowing any chance to help them become better. If our kids aren't getting it done in the classroom, *we're* failing on *their* behalf, not the other way around. Too often as teachers, we expect them to conveniently come to us, rather than committing to them and meeting them where their needs are and taking the steps of that educational journey with them. Most kids will complete that journey with us, and some of them ultimately won't, but all of them will learn something along the way.

We can't take the easy-way-out, one-size-fits-all, "shut up and play!" approach with our kids and expect it to work. We must find a way to help them understand *how* doing something in this way or that will benefit them. We must find a way to *connect* with them, to develop common ground, to let them know we care and that we're all in this together. When kids feel like we're talking *with* them, not just talking *to* them, when they realize we're trying to be a *teammate* instead of an *opponent*, they're able to let their guard down and begin to trust us. And once that trust is established, special things start to happen.

It's important to me that kids make it *to* college but, more importantly, that they make it *through* college once they arrive. Being at the door is a good start, of course, but charging through it and making the most of what's inside and *finishing* is key.

The number of games I won or lost as a coach never mattered much to me, so long as I knew we were doing things the right way, that I was helping kids to develop a game plan focused on teamwork and building character and learning to become part of something bigger than themselves; that I was helping them make it *to*, and *through*, college, to put themselves in position for life success. As a teacher and coach, my duty is the same: to try to help steer kids through the maze of stumbling blocks and mixed messages so prevalent during the transition from teenager to adult, to help them understand that achievement in life is about much more than chasing money or accumulating "things." Unfortunately, the only question that seems to matter in our society nowadays is, *How much will it cost me, and how much money can I make?* Our values seem to be based on immediacy and convenience, not on anything lasting. It's important to help kids understand they can become a part of something special and lasting.

Coaches who care only about winning games aren't concerned with silly things like life lessons for kids or preparing players to succeed off the court; the only education they're involved in is helping players graduate to the nearest street corner, stripped of skill and ill-equipped to handle what's ahead in life.

Ultimately, education shouldn't be about teaching kids *what* to think; it should be about teaching them *how* to think for themselves, to size up their situation, accept accountability for their choices and examine their options. Whether coaching or teaching, the mission is the same: trying to connect the dots of understanding for kids about why learning is important, about utilizing the lessons they learn to improve their lives and impact their teammates in a positive way.

The mission is to help them understand that, on and off the court, *we play the game the way we live our lives*. The way we think and talk and act each day will show itself in our roles as students or teammates or employees. It will impact our ability to be good husbands or wives or fathers or mothers down the road. We can't live a lie, acting one way "out there" and another "in here" and expect to succeed. The decisions we make on a consistent basis, good or bad, tell the truth about where we're headed. It's called karma.

For any of us, the ability to take an honest look at our decisions and the ripples they cause in our lives, and the lives of our teammates, is key. Instead of our typical *"Woe is me!"* refrain when things don't go our way, how about asking ourselves, "Why *was* it me, and *what is the lesson* God wants me to learn from the experience?" How about sidestepping our tendency to feel sorry for ourselves or blame others and take a deeper look at the part we played in creating our circumstances?

It's the same way when things are going well for us. When things are happening just right, when we're really on a roll, we must continue to try to improve, to fine-tune, to find ways to help our teammates get on a roll, too. We can't afford to get selfish, thinking it's all about us and that our teammates can fend for themselves. We can't get complacent, believing we've found all the answers and there is nothing left to learn.

Real education means we're *always* learning. And like it or not, one way or another, others are always learning from *us*, from our triumphs and troubles. The decisions we make and the ripples they cause, either positive or negative, are examples for others to study and emulate or avoid.

Our attitude about education will lead us to our potential or leave us behind. If we're always learning and applying that understanding, we're headed for good places. But if we're unwilling to enroll and we're indifferent to instruction, our journey will never begin. It's up to us.

With my granddaughter, Jaden. Winning where our kids' futures are concerned should always be the most important thing.

AFTERWORD

by Jared Sullinger

As a basketball player, I've learned a great deal from my father over the years about the fundamentals of the game, about those pieces that have to be in place for any player or team to realize their potential and succeed consistently during crunch time on the court. Those lessons have helped me to become the player I am today, and to understand what is necessary for me to be the best teammate I can be and make the most of the wonderful opportunity I have received to play at the professional level.

More important to me, however, are the lessons I've learned from him about what it takes to succeed in the biggest game there is: life. Some of those lessons I've learned more quickly than others. Some of those lessons have taken longer for me to understand, and have come with a higher price. Unfortunately, I was involved in a recent off-the-court situation that brought embarrassment to me and my family. I regret that I momentarily let my guard down and found myself in a position where my character could possibly be called into question, even if only temporarily. That experience, while humbling for me, only reinforced the importance of adhering to my father's message about doing the right things, for the right reasons, *consistently*...on and off the court. While thankful that I have been able to turn my attention and focus back to doing whatever possible in my role to help our team succeed, I learned a valuable lesson from that experience that I'll carry with me and believe will make me a better man because of it.

After all, my father taught me that, for any of us, it's not so much the adversity we face itself, but rather the way we *respond* to that adversity, that defines us, and I plan to respond with my best.

He taught me that, no matter how talented we may be at anything, our talent will get us nowhere without the proper effort and attitude. He's always said that even though there are many things in life we can't control, we can always control our effort and our attitude. Effort and attitude are the separator between those who become their best, and those who don't. He taught me that effort and attitude can't be a sometimes thing, that we owe the game our best each time we take the floor. Otherwise, we're cheating the game and ourselves. We're cheating all the greats who worked so hard while paving the way for us, guys like Bob Cousy and Bill Russell and Michael Jordan and countless others, who always gave their best, no matter what.

I continue to learn from my father what accountability, on and off the court, really means. Growing up, I used to hear one phrase from him more than any other: *You Play the Game the Way You Live Your Life*, he'd say. Basically, it means that the decisions we make off the court have a direct impact on our ability to perform on the court; that the way we handle our business away from the game, good or bad, will be reflected in how we react when the game is on the line. It means we can't let ourselves fall into bad habits, that we can't keep taking shortcuts in life and expect to succeed. We may get away with it for a while, but eventually, karma will come calling and it'll cost us when it matters most.

I learned that lesson the hard way while playing for my father at Northland High School. I was a nationally-acclaimed player, and I started to think I had all the answers. On the surface, I thought I was a great teammate, but my actions didn't support it. I didn't realize that being the best teammate I could be meant taking care of my business the right way off the court, too. While I was giving the game of basketball everything I had, I was letting my schoolwork slide. I had fallen into a habit of turning in class assignments late and making excuses for it. I thought that because I was playing well on the court, nothing else mattered. My father thought otherwise.

He suspended me for a crucial tournament game, a game we ended up losing. My poor decision-making off the court had cost my teammates in a big way. I had let them down, and I was crushed. Though it hurt him to suspend me for the game, as a coach and a father, he refused to allow me to disrespect the game by not handling my duties in the classroom. He wasn't interested in winning the wrong way. He was concerned about helping a young man learn a crucial life lesson, something that went far beyond basketball.

My father's decision to suspend me for that game was a huge wakeup call for me. It helped me understand that the selfish way I had been approaching things wasn't gonna get me far in life. It helped me understand that our decisions impact others, too, so we'd better make the right ones. It helped me understand that we're responsible for holding ourselves accountable, that it's about our actions, not our intentions, and excuses are unacceptable.

While I wish my suspension for that game hadn't been necessary, it taught me to never take the game for granted, to always respect it. That experience turned me around in the classroom, too. It made me get serious about my studies, and I became a better student.

Total commitment to our teammates is what it's always been about for my father. He expects nothing less. He taught me that, no matter how good a player we may be, none of us can do it alone, without help from our teammates. I learned from him that being a great player isn't about racking up individual stats. It's about finding ways to make our teammates better, about each of us using our skills to support each other, which helps the whole team succeed. It's about embracing our roles within the team concept, trying to become our personal best so we can help our teammates improve.

It's about everybody working together, playing with purpose for maximum benefit of the group. It's about synergy. He helped me understand that winning consistently requires contributions from the whole cast.

My father is far from perfect. Like anyone else, he has made his share of mistakes in life, and has accepted ownership of them. He has tried to use the lessons he's learned along the way to help others, especially kids, prepare for the challenges life throws at us. As a coach, wins and losses have never been the most important thing to him. His focus has always been on the best interests of the kids, on helping them learn to become a part of something bigger than themselves, on preparing them for life beyond basketball or sports. His focus has been on helping them understand the importance of fundamentals like teamwork and discipline and respect and humility to our success in life, no matter what we do.

To me, he is the blueprint for what a father should be. He lives by the rules, and he backs up his words with action. He's always been there for me and my family, no matter the situation, and I'm grateful to him for it.

ACKNOWLEDGMENTS

I'd like to thank many without whom this book would not have been possible.

To Barbara Sullinger and Kim Dauphin, thank you for your understanding and patience throughout this project.

To John, thank you for your sincerity from the time we decided to "do this thing." I believe fate is God's way of staying anonymous, and our paths crossing was meant to be.

Special thanks to Bob Snodgrass, publisher at Ascend Books, for believing in this project, allowing us the opportunity and providing invaluable guidance along the way.

Thanks to Beth Brown, publications coordinator at Ascend Books, for your kindness and keeping us on the path.

Thanks to Bob Ibach, Cheryl Johnson and Cindy Ratcliff for helping to make *Winning with Purpose* happen.

Thanks, also, to Thad Matta and John Beilein. Though NCAA guidelines prohibited your participation in this project, I value your belief and support.

Thanks to the late Vince Chickerella, the tremendously successful longtime high school coach in Columbus, for taking me under his wing and telling me he believed in me when I got my first head coaching job at East High School.

Thanks to all the players, coaches, parents and kids out there who believe in the value of winning the right way, who understand it means pushing aside our ego and using our skills to make those around us better, that it means working with purpose to impact others in a positive and lasting way, far beyond the next big game.

Lastly, thanks to my Grandpa Jim and Pat Penn, my coach at Oberlin College, for teaching me what winning with purpose in life is all about.

John would like to thank his wife, Kim, and his daughters, Alexa and Averi, for their belief and encouragement.

ABOUT THE AUTHORS

John Dauphin and Satch Sullinger
(photo courtesy of Annette Simon)

Satch Sullinger is a longtime coach, teacher and believer in the power of playing with purpose, on and off the court. Sullinger is the 2010 Naismith National High School Basketball Coach of the Year and father of Jared Sullinger, a member of the NBA's Boston Celtics and former All-American at The Ohio State University, where he led the Buckeyes to the 2012 Final Four. Jared Sullinger won the Naismith National High School Player of the Year award, also in 2010. The Sullingers are the only father and son to be named Naismith National Coach and Player of the Year, respectively. Sullinger was selected to coach in the Adidas Nations Global Championship in Los Angeles in 2012. The tournament features the top high school basketball players from around the world. Sullinger continues to speak at coaches' and youth clinics across the country.

John Dauphin has written for *The Plain Dealer, The Columbus Dispatch* and *Hittin' the Note*. He has interviewed and written about Bob Knight, B.B. King, Willie Nelson, Walter Cronkite, Roy Williams, Roger Clemens and Cameron Crowe. Crowe, the Oscar-winning writer and director of *Jerry Maguire* and *Almost Famous*, noted Dauphin's "powerful written voice." John wrote and directed *Winning Lives: The Story of Ted Ginn Sr.*, a documentary that aired on *CBS Sports Network*. *Winning Lives* is the inspirational story of the high school football coach and his efforts to make a positive impact on the turbulent lives of inner-city kids in Cleveland and beyond. John lives in Columbus with his wife and two daughters.

Visit www.ascendbooks.com for more great titles
on your favorite teams and athletes.

www.ascendbooks.com

DATE DUE